I0463063

# Unleash Your Inner Entrepreneur

## Know Whether to Build or Buy Your Perfect Business in 7 Simple Steps!

Randy Baker

## DISCLAIMER

# Dedication

To Laura,

Who sees me as I am and loves me anyway; who always encourages me to fearlessly step into my purpose, and without whom this book would not have been possible.

I love you.

# Table of Contents

1. TO BUILD OR BUY? THAT IS THE QUESTION!          5

2. WILL YOU LET ME BE YOUR GUIDE?                  12

3. SYSTEMS MAKE THINGS SO MUCH EASIER.             20

4. WHERE WILL YOUR BUSINESS TAKE YOU?              26

5. WHERE ARE YOU TODAY?                            38

6. BUILDING YOUR PERSONAL BLUEPRINT                50

7. CREATE FINANCIAL STABILITY                      62

8. IT IS NOT JUST A FINANCIAL DECISION             77

9. DO YOU BUY IT – OR BUILD IT?                    93

10. THE SEARCH BEGINS                              107

11. SUPERCHARGE YOUR SUCCESS                       122

12. BE THE ACTION HERO                             129

THANK YOU                                          139

# 1. To Build or Buy? That Is the Question!

I bet you have wanted your own business for a long time. Am I right? Were you the kind of kid who wanted to run a lemonade stand to make a few cents? Maybe you mowed lawns or washed dishes? Maybe you put yourself through high school by flipping burgers or selling magazine subscriptions?

Whatever it was that you did, and whether it was for extra money or because you needed to live, you found a way to do it. You went out and found a way to get the cash you needed or wanted. You did not just sit at home in front of the TV or game console, wishing things were different. You took action and got results.

And the bug took hold. You were born to own your own business. You knew deep inside that your life purpose was to own your own business. You probably read business magazines during college, and perhaps you took business classes. You loved to talk with local business owners and loved to think about how to make businesses work.

**Does this describe you?**

Maybe you were *not* that person. Maybe you were less passionate, but now that you are in the workforce, those nudges seem to be coming. You may be feeling that there is more to life than sitting on a help desk twenty-four hours a day. You may be thinking your boss is dumb as a box of rocks and that you can do better than that. Your career may have stagnated…you were passed over for the last couple of promotions, and it is clear you need to look at something different. If you are in these categories, what you are feeling inside – that urge that something is not right – is probably your inner entrepreneur looking to find a way out and to shine as only you can shine when you are in step with your inner being.

Or, maybe, you are older and have been "aged out" of your career. And now, you cannot find a way back in? (As a side note, did you know that the fastest growing demographic for entrepreneurs right now are people aged between fifty-five and sixty-five? These are people with great experience and knowledge who have been cast aside by a society that values youth over knowledge, so they start their own successful businesses. Their success rate is significantly higher than that of younger people. This tells a story, right?).

For most people, business ownership remains nothing more than a dream. They start to believe that it is a fantasy that is reserved for only those who are blessed with money or born into the right family (the lucky sperm club) or have advanced college degrees; or, they convince themselves of some other reason that tells them they can't do it.

I was nearly ten years into my first career as a chartered accountant when I was passed over for a promotion to partner of one of the biggest accounting firms in the world, KPMG. Now, I am not complaining at all. The time I spent there allowed me to travel the world, work on two continents, and really learn the basics of business. Then, the axe dropped. It was made perfectly clear that my career at KPMG was not only limited but likely to be short-lived.

This was a shock. I had just purchased an old house (built in 1887) and was in the process of renovating it to a livable state. My wife was pregnant with our first child and had literally just stopped working. The logical thing to do was to find another job, right?

But I couldn't do that. The entrepreneurial itch that I had managed to control for the previous ten years roared back with a vengeance. I could no longer tell myself that a career as a chartered accountant was my purpose – that was simply a lie I told myself to keep everybody happy. I had no choice. I had to become a business owner.

I started searching for a business to buy, so I connected with the business brokers in the local area. I did not think about how I was going to fund a new business. My mortgage and the costs of the renovation ate all our money…and we still had a baby coming. But that didn't stop my thirst for a business.

I spent hours and hours looking at possible product ideas for a business I could start myself. It was all too hard. Fears and doubts started entering my mind, a state of anxiety that I had never experienced before. I started to wonder what my family and friends would think. I started wondering if I even had the skills needed to run and manage a business. And what happens when the money runs out?

It took me some time to realize that I was simply finding excuses for not taking the plunge and actually doing something. What I was doing was not only spinning my wheels in the dirt of fear and worry; I was putting my sanity at risk, not to mention the well-being of my wife and our unborn child. Pretty selfish of me, right?

Imagine me, when a moment of frustration saw me with pen and paper in hand, listening to 70's rock music, and starting a list. The list contained all the things that were getting in the way of following my inner entrepreneur and owning my own business:

- I don't know whether to buy an existing business or start my own

- I don't know what product/service I want to provide

- I don't know how to buy a business

- I don't know what I need to do to start a business

- What if I fail?

- How do I pay for it?

- What will my wife think if it fails?

- What about my family?

- What about my friends?

- Where do I start?

- What do I need to do first?

- How do I build a plan?

The list of questions and excuses overflowed to a second page. Truthfully, it was demoralizing. It was just unanswered questions with no solutions. The exercise was far from fun, and the conclusion far from positive. I just started to feel overwhelmed and had no idea where to start in this process toward business ownership. So, I started looking for a regular job again.

But I would have given anything if someone had come along and said, "We can find a way through this. We can find a way for you to know whether to build or buy, what products are best for you, and what type of business is perfect for you."

I think I would have given that person rights to my first born! But I didn't know where to turn at the time. It was far easier to go the safe way; to stuff that itch in a bag and hide it under the bed, hoping it never surfaces again, and go get a job. But I learned something important through this process – something I suspect you are feeling right now.

## That Itch Always Comes Back

Have you experienced that yet? Have you tried to hide it away, lock it up in the deepest recesses of your mind, and yet it finds a way to appear again (usually at the worst possible time!)? Have you tried to ignore it? How did that work out for you?

I believe very strongly that entrepreneurs and businesspeople are not necessarily created, they are not made, and they are not a function of society. I believe people are born with a purpose, and, for some, that is to become business owners. The inner entrepreneur will never rest until it is fed, and its appetite for business is insatiable. It is this inner entrepreneur that is driving you to think about becoming a business owner. Can you feel it, right now? This very minute? Is it telling you to listen to these words as you read them…telling you that this is the path you were born to travel?

I know that feeling well. I also know the fear that sits in the pit of your stomach, slowly churning, looking for a way to tell you that what you are doing is crazy. I know the internal struggle you are dealing with. Your heart and soul are telling you to find a way to business ownership, while your brain (which has one job – to keep you alive) is telling you that it is too dangerous and providing evidence of the potential pitfalls.

I have had a long and exciting career in business, but it has taken a long time for me to understand that the way to business success (and therefore the way to overcome the almost paralyzing effect of fear) is to create a *process*. A process can be a simple system that walks you, step by step, through the decisions that you need to make while you prepare for business ownership.

You need a process that will make decisions easier, builds confidence, and answers the question of whether to build or buy your business. You need a process that supports you, the individual with the drive to succeed, and allows you to build the confidence to know you can and will succeed in your business.

This book will give you that process. It will walk you through the aspects you need to know in the right order. By following this simple process, forty years in the making, you will know in a few short weeks:

- Whether to build a business from scratch, or buy an existing one

- What products/services are best for your business

- What type of business is most suitable for you

- How to start the process of finding the right business to buy

- How to start the process of building your own business

You will get the most out of this book if you do not just read it and then put it on the shelf, never to be opened again. I highly recommend you journal your thoughts and opinions as you work through the book. Of course, doing the suggested exercises will bring success much faster than just thinking about them.

It is my wish that you will finish this book, and punch holes in the air with your fist because now you know without doubt that you can and will be a business owner. Your inner entrepreneur has become your best friend, and your life purpose translates to a life with purpose when you embrace it.

**Enjoy your journey. It starts here.**

*Have a question for me? Send me your ideas, comments and complaints. I want to know what you think. You can reach me at:*

*IAmNotFinished.com/contact-us*

# 2. Will You Let Me Be Your Guide?

I was young and dumb in the summer of '74, full of piss and vinegar and armed with my 1965 Holden car and fifty dollars of cash. I drove 3000 miles north with three friends, and when we arrived in Cairns with our money spent, we refused to give our parents the right to say, "I told you so." So, we became entrepreneurs instead.

We spent the next eight weeks spearfishing off the coast for any kind of fish we could catch, then hocking them in local RV parks to raise gas money for our return journey. We slowly moved down the coast, edging toward home, and succeeding (one fish after another) because we had no other choice.

My alternative journey into the business world had started. And my inner entrepreneur had awoken. It would take another twelve years or so before I would listen to it, and you know that story. Over the next thirty or so years, I started several businesses of my own. I discovered I had skills with start-ups and used those skills as the CFO of several start-ups. I was also involved behind-the-scenes at the birth of three brand new industries.

I know the struggles you face when buying or starting a business. I know first-hand the stresses and pressures that knock your confidence and threaten to tear your dream to shreds right in front of your eyes. I have seen and made the mistakes that beginner entrepreneurs all too often make. And I know that your inner entrepreneur can be a PITA (pain in the ass) sometimes, especially once it has decided that you are receptive to its nudges. Most importantly, I know what success looks and feels like. I know the thrill of achieving something important, of doing something hard and of being at the bleeding edge of new industries.

My advice for you? Don't settle for the ordinary. If you want something extraordinary, go out and get it. Do what you need to do to get there, and don't shy away from hard work or effort. Change is difficult but the rewards are amazing...

## "All Systems are *Go*"

The calm voice crackled in my earphones as I shifted uncomfortably in my seat; the parachute strapped to my back and forming part of my seat did little to calm my nerves. I could feel the adrenaline building inside me as a single bead of sweat rolled down my forehead and into my eye.

Looking to my left, I could see Colonel Richard (Rick) Searfoss; confident, collected, as he went through the pre-flight checklist. I was thankful that I was in the hands of this experienced pilot and astronaut, who had completed three shuttle flights and served as a US Navy Test Pilot in another life prior to joining us as our test pilot.

And there I was, sitting in the right seat; flight test engineer for this test flight of the X-Racer, a modified hand-built Velocity aircraft. The Velocity had originally been built with a conventional piston engine fitted to the rear of the vehicle. The Velocity I was sitting in today did not have a conventional engine. It had been removed, and in its place was a 2600 lb. thrust rocket engine, running on a mix of kerosene and liquid oxygen.

The kerosene was stored in the original fuel tanks within the wings of the plane. The liquid oxygen (lox) was stored in a tank immediately behind our seats. The rear seats had been removed to enable installation of the tank. For all intents and purposes, this was akin to riding a highly explosive bomb ... bareback.

But there I was strapped in, waiting, as I heard the countdown. "3...2...1...ignition."

It was too late to get out now.

I had no choice.

My heart beat rapidly in my chest, my breathing irregular, as my hands curled into tight fists; as time *stopped*.

"We have ignition", I heard the Colonel say. I looked at the console dashboard, where I could see the rocket engine roar into life, spitting blue, yellow, and red flames behind us.

My job as flight test engineer was surprisingly simple ... I was expected to watch the flame from the engine. There was a camera mounted on the rear wing tips aimed at the engine, with a feed directly to the cockpit. I was to inform the Colonel of *any* abnormality I saw in the flame as we conducted the flight test.

The plane rapidly gained speed as it literally rocketed down the runway, bouncing and shaking like it was trying to tear itself to pieces...or perhaps it was trying to outrun the forces that propelled it?

After what seemed an eternity (but was really only about 13 seconds) the plane lifted from the runway.

We rotated to the right and pointed our nose to the heavens.

The sky was deep blue with nary a cloud.

And appeared endless.

My entire body was pushed backwards into the seat, the thrust from the rocket engine continuing to accelerate us through the air as we went higher and higher. The rattling reduced to a level of vibration that was scary but not as horrifying as it had been. I took my eyes off the engine flames for a moment and glanced out the window ... we were already eight or nine thousand feet up, with no sign of slowing down.

The noise of the engine permeated the earphones as a loud thrum and penetrated our bones in a similar way a deafening subwoofer might.

And then, suddenly, nothing.

I was thrown forward in my seat, caught by the full harness seat belts.

Acceleration stopped dead.

Noise was replaced by silence.

Glancing at the monitor in front of me, I saw a flicker of blue and orange as the flames died. The left side of the plane dipped violently as the pilot sent it into a rapid barrel roll.

Before I knew it, we were flying inverted ... heads pointed groundward before the roll was completed. And we were right side up once more.

"3 ... 2 ... 1 ... ignition," came the colonel's voice once more. Again, the engine fired up, a long trail of flames shooting out, the shock diamonds (blue diamonds that can be seen in the flames when the rocket engine is running efficiently) visible on the monitor I was watching.

In seconds we were again facing straight up, shooting into the endless sky under rocket power. I was now enjoying the adventure. The adrenaline had done its work. I tried to remember a time when I had felt so alive as I did at that moment.

Again, the engine was turned off ... and again relit.

Shutting a rocket down in flight and re-lighting it in flight was a huge technological advancement, and one that differentiated our company from the few competitors in our field. As we coasted back to the runway in the Mojave desert, the heat haze shimmering below us, the plane buffeted by the strong breeze that had sprung up seemingly from nowhere, and my job being done, I could now spare a moment to think about how I – a finance guy, an accountant, a marketing guy – could have found himself sitting in the right seat of a rocket-powered airplane, doing the job of flight test engineer.

I am guessing that there are fewer than five hundred people alive today who have flown in a rocket plane of any sort. And here I was, about to land on a little airstrip in the desert, having flown in an experimental rocket vehicle.

Looking back to that day, more than a decade ago, and thinking about my journey in life, there are a few small, simple insights I have obtained that I think would be worthy of sharing.

We often think about journeys as being arduous, hard, perhaps even a test of our courage. This can be true, but the journey should also (and perhaps more importantly) be filled with adventure, fun, and enjoyment. It should ultimately allow you to look back and love the life you have lived.

Journeys may have an element of risk, an indeterminate destination, or even no destination. But the best journeys are those where there are direction, objectives, and broad-stroke goals. Bobbing meaninglessly like an empty bottle on the ocean, driven by wind and tide, may be a journey in life. However, it will result in life determining what happens *to* you, rather than you being in control of your *own* direction.

Fun and adventure await those who follow their hearts, especially if you also do the work. Take the steps necessary to allow opportunity to come knocking…if you are brave enough to answer the call.

I shared this story simply to show that the life of the entrepreneur, the life of the businessperson, is a journey that they can control, a journey with a destination, and steps to that destination. My career has been exciting. My business ownership, on several occasions, has been an adventure with a destination. I have intermingled business ownership with helping other entrepreneurs build great businesses in new industries.

I was in the internet industry building a search engine when everyone was saying nobody was ever going to use email regularly. That company completed an IPO about two years after starting and reached a valuation in excess of six billion!

I was in the New Space industry when everyone was saying that no one but governments could ever afford to build rockets and fly to space. Elon Musk proves them wrong all the time…and we tested Elon's first rocket engine!

Most recently, I was involved in the cryptocurrency industry. While it remains too early to know whether cryptocurrency will be a success, the underlying blockchain technology is changing the world as we know it and over the next few years will have an incredible impact on many industries.

This can be the life of the business owner, the life of the entrepreneur.

## Get to Your Destination

In the previous chapter, I shared with you what happened when I was forced out of KPMG. My inner entrepreneur came forward, demanding attention. I was exactly where you are today. I left that story at the point when I gave up and started searching for a job.

But that is not where the story ends. With support from my wife, I stopped searching for full time work and started a part time job delivering pizza while I searched for a business to build or buy. Opportunity comes when risk is taken, and, in this case, I found opportunity while driving.

My first business was a dinner delivery service in Melbourne, Australia. We delivered meals from some of the best restaurants in Melbourne to customers in their own homes. This was an early version of Uber Eats or Favor, long before those businesses existed.

I listened to and accepted my inner entrepreneur and took action. I became a business owner. Some of the lessons learned in that process form the steps in the process that I lay out carefully in this book. The systems and procedures taught here have come from what I have actually done. They have been tried and tested over time, many times. They have been changed, refined, and made as simple as possible for you to learn.

Most importantly, they are the same processes that I use in my own life, my own businesses, and those of my clients. They will work for you, too. But you need to put in the effort. We do not have a silver bullet that magically makes this process easy. Simple, yes. Easy? Not so much.

I was not always successful. I had failures, particularly early in my business ownership career. I got things wrong. I learned from them. I developed this system to reduce my risk; to give me the best chance of success in my business and those of my clients. It worked for us, and it will work for you, too.

It is time to stop spinning your wheels and start taking positive action, with a plan and a process that gets you to your destination. Want to fly in a rocket? Put in the work up front, and then anything is possible!

# 3. Systems Make Things So Much Easier.

OK, so here is a simple fact for you to digest. You just have to walk into a book store or go onto Amazon and glance at the business book section, and you will be inundated with literally hundreds of books that claim to be able to show you how to start, build, or grow your business.

Many of these books will have clever titles designed to catch your attention. Many will be written by twenty- and thirty-something-year-old's who have found success in their own business experience. Some will have useful information. A few will have ideas that are new and interesting. Many of these books are well worth reading if you want to stuff your head with knowledge, ideas, and thoughts.

But if you want to succeed in business – if you truly want to know the secrets to success – you need to look past the youngsters and find an experienced coach to *guide* you. You don't need someone to tell you what you should do just because it worked for them. No two businesses are alike, and no solution fits all problems.

The art that is business ownership or entrepreneurship is *not* a list of what to do, what to try, or what not to do. The art is found in the way you think. The magic can be found in the way you systematize your thinking and the way you build processes in your mind.

There are always many ways to do something. There are many right ways. The business owner magician is the one who is able to see the impact his decisions make on other aspects of his business. To do this, he breaks every problem down into small, bite-sized chunks and, like a jig-saw puzzle, examines how all the pieces fit.

Over the last four decades, I have developed a process that does exactly that. It will build the mental muscles and the brain power that will help you adapt this process to any situation you come across.

Business is not a set of pre-determined steps that you follow. It is not a dance routine that you can learn and, after memorizing the steps, can repeat at will. It is more like a freestyle downhill ski race, where every bump, every turn creates opportunity for creativity and challenge, while you are racing downhill at ever-increasing speeds.

How can you possibly maintain control in that environment? Certainly not by relying on predetermined dance steps! So, with that in mind, you are going to learn a process that trains your brain to think like a true entrepreneur.

I know that the biggest question you want to solve today is whether you should buy an existing business or start one from scratch. This is indeed a very important question to answer, and it is the question you must answer before taking that first step toward business ownership.

But…There are many more questions that need to be answered before you can actually answer that one! The system I have created will walk you step-by-step through the process; building the strong foundation you will need for success and answering the question of whether to buy or build. In the process, you will identify the best product(s) for you and the best business type.

## The Business Ladder System

Let me be very clear. This is the exact system I use when I think about my own businesses, and it is the same tool I use to solve problems, create new products, and build plans. Its very simplicity, once understood, allows you to dissect questions and find solutions quickly and efficiently. After some time, you will possess an automatic response to problem resolution at your fingertips.

Make no mistake, this is a very powerful system. Once mastered, it will make you wonder why it is not taught anywhere else. So, what can you expect as you work through this book?

You will be challenged to think differently about many aspects of business life. You will be challenged to look at yourself with complete honestly. You will be challenged to envision your destination, and you will be given the tools to map your own path to that destination.

I have broken the Business Ladder System down into seven rather simple steps. Each step has been designed to be simple to recall, but there is a great deal of brain work required by you to make sure you remain on the right path, moving forward in a systematic and logical way. Each step builds on the solid foundation of the previous step, moving you closer to understanding what is best for you and how to make the right decisions.

This is not my exercise; it is yours. The more thought and effort put into each step in the process, the better the final outcome. Some clients like to keep a journal or take notes of their thinking as they work through the steps. Many find that their thinking may change as they progress, and some find it very valuable to refer to their notes as a way to remind them of why they came to the conclusions they did. I strongly recommend this approach. So, let's look at the steps and see where they lead:

### Step 1: Look Forward to Your Destination

This step is essential to knowing where you are going. In this step, you will identify where you want to be at the end of this journey.

### Step 2: Ask Where You Are Now, Today

You will honestly evaluate where you are today. This step becomes the starting point of your journey, and the next five steps will bridge the gap between today and the future.

### Step 3: Design Your Personal Blueprint

You will examine why you need a personal blueprint, a personal plan. You will start the process of mapping out that plan.

### Step 4: Decide To Treat Money With New Respect

You will discover a new way to think about money. You will take an honest look at your current financial situation and create a plan to immediately reduce any financial stress, as well as a simple system to ensure personal financial stress does not inhibit business success. The blue print you create for financial stability uses the same thinking that you will use when running your new business.

### Step 5: Examine Non-Financial Needs

You will learn that business ownership is affected by several other non-financial aspects. You will build personal blueprints to manage relationships, health, education, your beliefs, and passions. This step will enable you to create balance in your life today that you will be able to retain once you have either bought or started your new business.

### Step 6: Respond To Your New Knowledge

You will bring all the information you have gathered in the previous five steps together and learn how they will drive your decisions about the products or services, and the business type that is best suited to get you to the destination you imagined in Step 1. The personal blueprints that you have developed will give you the answers you need to be able to make great decisions about the future. You will then be able to identify whether you should buy your business, or whether you really want to build it from scratch. To make this decision without first going through this process could lead you to the wrong solution and possibly failure as an entrepreneur.

### Step 7: Start the Search

In this super exciting step of the process, you will examine how to go about starting the process of buying or building your new business. You will discover ways to reduce the cost of buying your new business and will learn the mindset that is most essential if you are building your business from scratch.

By the time you have completed Step Seven, you will be fully prepared to become a business owner. You will have put in place the plans, procedures, and thought processes that will guide you as you run your business, grow it, and enjoy the many benefits of business ownership.

You will know how to avoid many of the mistakes most business owners make, how to create quick plans to simplify any problem (hint: it is the same as every blueprint you build during this process) and keep your personal finances stable and healthy.

I urge you to follow the process in the order I have laid out for you. At times, it may seem that you are not moving forward, and the temptation to jump ahead to the section you *really* want to read may be great. After all, we sometimes think that we know what is being said and don't need to hear any more. That may be right, but it may equally be wrong.

Many years of experience have created the foundation for this system. It is designed to tackle and deal with those things that create stress first and to build on the freedom that reduction in stress can provide. Each building block supports the next, and the journey itself will be one of self-discovery for you.

When approached with an open heart, a clear mind and an honest assessment, this system will break down barriers, reduce fears, and provide you with confidence. You will believe that you are not only fully prepared for business ownership but have the necessary skills and knowledge to be successful.

You can do this. Be brave, be confident, and be willing to challenge yourself, and the impossible can become possible. You can be a business owner and can know whether building or buying is best for you.

*Can you come up with a similar system? If it seems overwhelming, I'm happy to help. Reach out to me for a private discussion to map the outcome of your business at info@IAmNotFinished.com*

# 4. Where Will Your Business Take You?

The speakers above me crackled and a tinny voice could be heard saying, "Ladies and gentlemen, this is your captain speaking. We have been cleared for take-off. Would you please put away all electronic devices and make sure they are safely stowed? All cell phones must be turned off. Please put your seat backs up and your tray tables in the closed position. Our flight today will be a relatively short one. If your destination today is *not* business ownership, please let the stewards know and they will be pleased to provide sedatives for your comfort. Please, sit back, relax and enjoy this journey!"

Now, imagine you were sitting beside me.

I turn to you and start polite conversation as I often do with fellow travelers: "Hi, my name is Randy Baker, and I am going to be your guide as we go through this journey together. I am really excited that you are on board and ready to go! Do you mind if I ask you a few simple questions, so that I can have a better understanding of you and where you are at right now?"

You may say, "Sure! I am super excited to be starting this journey with you. Can't wait to get started!"

"Wait…you haven't started yet?"

You will then say, "Well…not really. I know I want to own my business, but…well, that is as far as I have gotten…is that OK? I mean, what should I have done?"

"Of course, that is ok…in fact, I truthfully prefer to work with people who have not yet made decisions about their business. They usually make wrong decisions that ultimately lead to failure. So, we are going to avoid that, and we are building a process together that will give you every chance of success."

We both gaze off into the middle distance…two travelers on the same journey, lost in their own thoughts as they wait to reach their future (which I know is already done for them – they just don't understand that yet).

Does the above scenario sound like you? Are you excited to be starting this journey but tentative at the same time? Are you wondering what the end result can be? Let me assure you that there is nothing at all to fear. During this journey you will challenge the way you have thought in the past and let go of anything that is in the way of your success. You will reinvigorate enjoyment of life, find financial stability, improve your relationships, find purpose, and live your passion. Who would have thought that you could have it all?

Don't get me wrong. The journey you have started is long and arduous. It may stretch you beyond what you ever thought capable of achieving. But the good news is that the proven process we are starting today will reduce risk, allow life balance, and drive you toward business ownership (and, more importantly, business success).

**So, let's get started.**

Every journey has a starting point and a destination. We know that today is your starting point. What we don't know yet is your destination. Until we can define your destination, we cannot define the steps to get there. Even more importantly, without a clear, well documented, and well understood destination, we cannot possibly get there. We will take wrong turns, get distracted by shiny objects, get tired, and give up. Or, we may even allow fear to enter our lives. We will listen to that small, inner voice that tells us we are not good enough, don't know enough, don't have enough money and a million other reasons that will prevent you from finishing.

When deciding to embark on business ownership, there are a few fundamental things you must "own," and the only place to start is the destination. I know, I have heard it many times. "Anybody can own a business." Or, maybe "Why don't you just fire your boss and start your own business? If he can do it, you sure can!"

I'm going to let you into a little secret here that very few people actually talk about. The failure rate of businesses is astonishing. One study recently indicated that 70% of businesses fail in their first year and less than 10% remain in business after five years. If anybody can do it, why so many failures?

I have a theory on this. I believe that entrepreneurs are born, not made. Successful business owners have a real need to go into business for themselves. Until they feed that need, their lives feel empty and unfulfilled. They have a desire to make the universe better, to provide value, and to change lives.

By contrast, most business owners go into business because they are "buying" a job. They may be unemployed, or their careers have stagnated, and they think owning a business will solve all their problems. The ugly truth is that without that internal drive to own a business, no amount of education, knowledge, or talent will lead to a successful business.

Do you have that insatiable need? Do you spend hours each day daydreaming about what it would be like if you could break the shackles of the 9 to 5 job? Do you know deep within your soul that you were born to be in business for yourself?

If you can answer 'yes,' to these questions, then congratulations! You are in the right place. I will nurture your inner entrepreneur, coaxing him to come out and play in a safe and creative environment; an environment that supports the crazy, celebrates the innovative, and builds businesspeople with vision, creativity, and a pathway to success.

Before we get too far in, I want to mention the major reason that businesses fail. It is usually not because the product or service is not good (although that is sometimes the case). It is usually a result of poor financial management, but not just within the business. It is poor personal financial management on the part of the owners; stress from that impacting relationships, health and motivation are the real culprits behind business failure.

Now, it is not the business owners' fault that this happens. Most business owners/entrepreneurs get into business without fully understanding that they need to be personally prepared before entering business. Very few can fix things after the event. It is not their fault that this happens. This stuff is not generally taught. The information you will discover in this book is challenging and unique, but is focused on *you* to ensure that you do not become a victim of your own business.

So, now that we know businesses fail mostly because of the owner's problems, what can we do to reduce that risk?

We start at the end.

**We start with the destination.**

Way back in 1983, I had the opportunity to travel throughout Africa. (I know, I am dating myself here – so it should come as no surprise that I am also addicted to 70's music!) The trip by four-wheel-drive army truck lasted around six months, starting at the southern tip of South Africa (Capetown) and working our way north to Morocco, across the Strait of Gibraltar, to Spain, and back to London.

It is fair to say that six months of sleeping in a small tent on the hard-packed ground certainly toughens your body, and spending that time with twenty strangers builds emotional strength. So, when we arrived in Arusha, Tanzania at the base of Mount Kilimanjaro, I was confident that I had the physical strength and stamina to make the climb to the top. In case you are not as familiar with Kilimanjaro, I should mention that the mountain is the tallest in Africa (at 19,341'). In 1983, it presented quite a challenge to the would-be climber. I am guessing that in the history of the mountain, up until 1983, maybe 2,000 people had made the climb. Now, in 2019, roughly that number of people climb it every year!

On the journey to Arusha, we could see the mountain in the distance, rising majestically above the plains of the Serengeti, its snow-covered summit beckoning, daring me to step foot on it. I knew at that moment that I had to accept that challenge. I knew in that first sighting of this mountain that I was going to climb it, that I was not going to succumb to altitude sickness, and that I was destined to reach the top.

I knew this as clearly as I knew my own name. I could see myself standing at the top of Africa and gazing out over the endless plains. My heart beat hard with excitement at just the thought of being there. My mouth became dry as I contemplated exactly what it would be like when I reached the summit.

My destination was clear. I could feel it in my soul. I could describe what I would feel like to anybody who cared to ask. I could literally see myself at the top.

The destination.

Start with the end.

When you think about business ownership, have you pictured your destination? Can you describe in detail what it would be like when you get there? Do you know how your life would be different?

I know you are asking questions like, "How do I know what the destination is when I don't even know what my business will be or when I can start it?" or, "How can I possibly know what my life will be like in the future? Nobody knows the future!"

And you would be right – nobody can know with certainty what the future holds. That is why you have the opportunity to make your destination exactly whatever you want it to be. Do you want ten million dollars? That's a destination. Do you want a big house, cars, or yachts? A destination. Do you want a happy life with your wife and three kids? Destination.

To help you determine *your* destination, I have put together a number of questions for you to answer. I find it helps to write down the answers rather than just reading and thinking. You may wish to refer to these answers later on as you read through this book. It is also OK if you don't have answers – this is a process and, as we work through it, many things will become clearer for you.

**Questions about your business plans.**

- What is the thing(s) that is driving you toward owning your own business?

- What do you want your business to achieve?

- Who do you think is your customer/client?

- What is your timeline to business ownership?

**Questions about you:**

- Why do you want a business? (Financial security, legacy, doing good, making a shitload of money, hate your boss, your career sucks, etc.)

- What do you define as success with your business?

- What does success mean to you? (Money, recognition, fame, etc.)

- Describe in detail what your life will be like when your business is successful (Where you live, type of house, cars you drive, bank account, kids, family, vacations, working hours, charity support/creation, etc. Be really detailed here. Make it so that you can feel it, taste it. This is your Kilimanjaro summit.)

- Describe in detail how you will feel when you reach that success?

You now know, without any doubt, what the destination is. You know what it looks like, you know what it feels like; you may even know what it tastes like and smells like. This is your Kilimanjaro summit. This is your big objective.

A quick word of warning here. Most people set their destinations with lower expectations than what is possible. This is not the time to think small. This is the time to be the largest person you can possibly be. This is the time to let your deepest wishes be seen, your truth that may have been suppressed in the past. Let yourself be free and think big, let your inner deepest needs surface. Nobody will see this but you, so there is no right or wrong answer. There is no limit to what you see as your destination.

We are looking for the best and greatest *you* to emerge and tell the universe what your destination is. Do not limit this exercise because you don't know how to get there from here. Right now, we are only looking for your destination – make it a big one!

Let's take a short detour back to the slopes of Kilimanjaro. The base camp for the climb was at around 6,500 feet altitude. Even there, I could feel the reduced oxygen levels. My breathing was a little sharper than normal, my body felt a little heavier, and I even started to have doubts that I could successfully make the climb. After all, if I was feeling lack of oxygen at 6500 feet, why did I think that I could breathe at 19,000+ feet?

The only thing that got me to the starting gate was remembering how I felt when I first saw the mountain. I admit that the thought of climbing around 13,000 vertical feet over the next two and a half days sent palpitations through my heart, made my legs weak, and nearly gave me reason to not even start. But I pushed forward.

Day 1 was a relatively short day. We climbed about 3,500 feet in a five-hour trudge through rain forest; up giant natural steps carved out of the mountain rock by centuries of water flow from melting snow. These steps were not your normal five-inch step...they were eighteen or twenty-four inches...and some required a full-body climb. It was exhausting, difficult, and tested every muscle in my body.

Reaching camp was a relief, and as I nursed my aching muscles, had a bottle of Safari beer (worst beer on the planet), and a few morsels of stew, my subconscious was telling me that I could not do this. It was telling me that I would fall off the side of the mountain in exhaustion and end up dead in some crevice, where my body couldn't be retrieved until the spring thaw next year. It was telling me I was too old, too weak, too pathetic... What did I think I was doing? It reminded me that I was an accountant, bland, boring...not an adventurer, not a mountain climber.

But there I was, sleeping in a wooden cabin with no heat, the wind howling through the numerous holes in the walls, the temperature plummeting well below freezing during the night. And I refused to let myself listen to those words of failure. I clung to the success I knew was coming.

Day two was much easier, but a very long day. It was more akin to a long uphill hike than a climb. After a quick breakfast, we set out at 8 a.m. and travelled about twelve miles, climbing another 4,000 vertical feet. No food awaited us when we arrived at the next shelter. It was straight to bed as we were starting day 3 at 12.30 a.m. in a race to the summit before the sun rose. At 14,000 feet, oxygen was scarce...truly. Breathing was difficult, and if it wasn't for physical exhaustion, no sleep would have come. As it was, when I was awakened at midnight after a couple of hours restless dozing, the cabin bitterly cold, limbs seemingly frozen, all I wanted to do was say, "I got here – that is success, that is good enough!"

But it wasn't. It wasn't the destination. It wasn't where I wanted to be.

And right then, a miracle happened.

My subconscious took on a new identity. Instead of saying, "You can't do this," it was saying, "You got this!"

The fears disappeared, and the self-doubt passed away. It was replaced by the smell of success, even though I was still seven hours of hard work away from the summit.

It was with renewed energy that I started the final push to the summit. As I climbed higher, the effects of altitude sickness started to hover around the edges of my consciousness. I watched in dismay as members of my party succumbed and turned back, passing me with nothing but failure and regret in their eyes.

I was standing on the top of the world (or at least Africa) when the sun crested the eastern horizon. I watched as the world awoke from its sleep. Taking a moment to thank the universe for the beauty it had offered me that morning, I then looked inward and discovered something I had known all along: if the destination is real enough to touch, to feel, to know in your soul, your inner strength will always be there to drive you to the finish. However, you must give it the space to do its work.

This is the lesson that I want you to understand. It is why the work on your destination is so important to your success. It is why your destination must be big, must be a stretch.

Your inner self needs room to do its work. The smaller the destination, the more limits you place on yourself.

Now would be a great time to go back and revisit the questions I asked earlier. It may be that you will want to refine your answers, or maybe not. It is totally up to you to define your destination…but remember this: the smaller your destination, the smaller your ability to achieve it. Weird, I know. But miracles happen when you give yourself space to work.

So, where do you want to go?

**Take action now.**

Draw a chart; the vertical axis can be named something like "happiness" or "success." The scale is simple from "today" at the bottom to "awesome" or "amazing" at the top. The horizontal axis is simply "time" with "today" at the left and "destination" at the right.

I want you to simply plot your "destination" mark on the upper right of the chart. This is the start of your process to business ownership. You know your destination. You know what it will feel like. You know why you are going there.

Keep this chart somewhere safe; we will be going back to it frequently as we continue to build your blueprint for business success.

Like many things in life, business success is a process, not an event. It does not just happen magically. It does not happen through luck (although some people are lucky for a short period of time). It is not the result of some sort of lottery where you draw the right card and you win. It does not come as a result of somebody else's failure.

Business success comes from following a process. It comes from getting all the right ducks in line. From taking a step by step approach to solving problems.

As we go through this process, it will be tempting to lose focus, or run ahead to the next chapter. You may want to even skip chapters that you don't think apply to you. I encourage you to avoid doing that, even if you think you know what I am going to say. Sometimes the key to knowledge can be found in the smallest comments.

We are building a process for *you*. It is yours to own, yours to manage, and yours to play with. Nothing is set in stone. You will find the way that works for you within the philosophy found here. The process is designed for long term success. That means that there may be some short term difficulties as we work through the process. Do not be discouraged if these raise their heads. A general philosophy I adopt throughout this process is that happiness can be found by making more of what you have rather than wanting more and not getting it.

Go ahead and plot your destination. You may wish to create a vision board, or have your destination printed. What you do with it is up to you, but I recommend that you keep it somewhere that you can refer to regularly. It is, after all, the objective for you in your business.

*If you would like me to guide you through a visualization of your destination, so that you can do a little space-time hopping, drop me a note at info@IAmNotFinished.com and we will arrange a time to get together. Just put "Destination" in the subject line!*

# 5. Where Are You Today?

The journey to business ownership starts today. You know the destination and can feel it in your very soul. You know where you are going; you know why you are going there, and you know what to expect when you get there.

Hang on a minute…how can you go there if you don't know where we are today?

The destination exercise we completed in the last chapter was based on making the future what you want it to be. It was based in creativity, dreams, desires, and needs. It was designed to make the future real for you and in some ways contained an element of fantasy that you want to make real. That is perfect for the future, and I applaud the greatness you identified.

But today we are doing something much, much more difficult.

Today we are going to deal with reality.

Today, there is no room for dreaming, no room for creativity. Today is dedicated to cold, hard truth. Reality has a way of putting to rest all creativity, of destroying hope for the future, and of limiting your future. But we need to go there…we need to find out who you are and where you are today.

I had a very interesting experience way back in eighth grade (I think the dinosaurs were still roaming the earth then). This experience must have had quite an impact, as I remember it like it was just yesterday.

My English literature teacher was a rebel. He wore long hair (not just a little too long – I am talking long enough to qualify him as a true hippie). He was the epitome of the hippie generation with his too-tight jeans, cheesecloth shirts, beads, and Jesus sandals. In fact, he was everything we impressionable early teens thought was cool and to be admired (if you lived through the 70's and can remember them, you know exactly who I am talking about!).

His teaching methods were as different as his attire. English Literature was supposed to be a curriculum based on the classic novelists and poets; a study in wordsmithing, literary sentence structure, grammar and beauty in writing.

That was not in store for our classes.

We studied things like lyrics to modern songs, studied books like *A Clockwork Orange* (it would be several years before I was old enough to see the movie by Stanley Kubrick). We studied "American Pie" by Don Maclean and songs by the Stones. We examined the influence of pop culture on modern society, and we compared music with art and novels. English Literature became our favorite class. It was the one class that we could actually make sense of, and the one that helped us understand the world. As a young teenager, this was the most impactful learning experience of my life and has stayed with me through the decades.

And then, one winter day, he came into class, sat his ass on the corner of a desk…and looked at each of us. The room was deathly quiet. We waited through this pregnant pause…a stillness full of promise, full of "the moment."

When he finally spoke…he posed a question:

"Imagine that there was a great flood. Water everywhere, the river had burst its banks and the town was flooded. You found refuge in a tree, where you were hanging on for dear life, but you were safe as long as you stayed tucked in its boughs. As you looked around, you saw an old man clinging to a branch and being swept away by the flood waters. You know he will not make it without help…but you are safe in your tree. What do you do? Do you ignore the cries for help and try to forget what you saw? Do you jump in and try to save him, knowing it could cost your life?"

He paused, taking a long look at each of us…"I don't want you to answer that question…at least, not today. What I want to tell you today is that, in life, you have one task. Just one thing and if I can teach you anything, it is this."

He stood and said softly, "That one thing is to know who you are."

Without another word, he walked to the door, opened it, and closed it gently behind him. He left the class, left the school, left our lives…and I never heard of him again. To be honest, I don't even remember his name, but I remember his words.

What I do know today is that his words on that day resonated with something deep inside of me. It took me a while to understand what he was saying…it took me thirty years to know the answer to his question (that is a story for another time), but there was no other lesson that I learned from that day forward that was more important.

## "That One Thing is to Know Who You Are"

You see, when you know who you are, deep down, without all the masks you wear and without all the trimmings that help us to appear to be the way you *want* to be, there remains the truth.

This part of the process to business ownership requires the same level of brutal honesty with yourself that is required for you to know who you are. I want you to be brutally honest with yourself as you answer the questions I will pose in a few minutes time. Let me warn you in advance that your inner voice will probably come out and tell you that, "You see, you can't be a successful businessperson – just look at the mess you are today!"

The good news is that this is exactly what we want to happen. Remember your destination? Remember how you will feel when you get there? Well, you can't get there without first knowing where you are today.

You may want to do this exercise in a quiet place; a place where you can reflect inwardly and that feels comfortable and safe. Nobody is going to see what you do here, except you. Grab a beverage, maybe a snack, and let's get this started.

Just like the destination exercise, it will help you immensely if you write down the answers to these questions. There may be some questions that you just don't have an answer to, and that is OK. Just move on to the next question.

Remember, to get the full benefit from this you need to be totally honest with yourself. Failure to be honest with yourself will simply make it far more difficult for you to create the right blueprint for your success. This is the first steppingstone to get you from this point to your destination.

**Personal Questions:**

- How do you feel right now? Excited? Angry? Tentative? Scared? Encouraged?

- How would you like to feel right now?

- What, in your mind, needs to happen for you to get from how you feel to how you would like to feel?

- Describe what will happen if you continue doing what you are doing and don't have your own business.

- Describe what will happen if you do get your own business, but it fails. What options do you have left?

**Financial questions:**

- Do you have any financial concerns? Are you under financial pressure?

- How long could you survive if you lost your income for any reason?

- Is your debt manageable today, or do you need to manage it better?

- Do you manage money well?

- Do you have any savings?

- Do you have large expenses coming up in the next 3 to 12 months? (i.e. planned vacations, house repairs, new cars, education expenses, etc.)

- What would you like to see happen financially?

**Relationship questions:**

- Are you in a committed relationship?

- If not, would you like to be?

- Does your partner know, understand, and support your need to become a business owner?

- Can your partner support you financially?

- Kids? Ages, sex, and plans for the future?

- Is your relationship with your partner where you want it to be? Could it be better?

- What is preventing it from being what you want it to be?

- Do you have strong bonds with family?

- Do you have a strong circle of friends? Are you the type who prefers a small group of close friends?

- What do your work colleagues think of you? Are you smart, fair, arrogant, etc.?

- What would you like to see in any/all of your relationships that is not there now?

**Business questions:**

- What are you good at doing?

- What do you like doing?

- Do these align with what you think your business should be?

- What business experience do you have?

- Why do you believe you can run a business?

- Do you know the difference between working on the business and working in the business?

- Have you managed staff before? Did you like it?

- Do you understand accounting? Do you understand P&L accounts, balance sheets, cash flow statements?

- Do you have any marketing experience? Sales knowledge?

- Will this business be your full-time job (even if it starts part time), or do you want to have a manager?

- Do you know what product/service you would like to offer?

- Do you know who your ideal customer is? Define him/her with as much detail as possible.

- Do you understand how to calculate costs?

- What do you believe you need to learn to be able to run your business properly?

I know this was a long list of seemingly unconnected or haphazard questions, but I assure you that an honest examination of where you are today will pay huge dividends as we progress deeper into this process. The obvious first benefit is that the answers to these questions will help you identify very clearly the work that will be needed as you continue this journey.

Business building is a process but preparing to be a business owner is where the foundation to business success can be found. This is the step that most people don't invest in.

The good news is that you will not look backwards after today. Every step in the process now is forward-looking. Where you are at today will no longer be the case tomorrow. If you identified areas for improvement in answering the questions, that will become part of your blueprint for success. Where you identified strengths, they will become the pillars of success that we will build on together.

I remember a time, not long after I started my first business, a dinner delivery service in Melbourne, Australia. I was sitting with my father watching Australian Rules football. If you have not seen it, take a look on YouTube and spend a few minutes watching it. It is a combination of full contact basketball, and football played on a field five times the size of an American football field. It is a fast, tough game that sometimes defies the laws of gravity. Take a look.

Anyway, my father's favorite team, the Essendon Bombers, were playing and losing badly. Now, my dad was a man of few words, but when he spoke, he usually had something of importance to share.

He was a small businessman and owned his own butcher shop. I can still remember him coming home from a hard day of work, the scent of his after shave masked almost entirely by the smell of meat; standing in the kitchen with his brown cardigan buttoned up, the bottom two unbuttoned and making him appear a little comical. He would come in and say something like, "Another slow day at the shop, but it will be OK," almost like clockwork before heading off to clean up for dinner.

Anyway, as we watched the football together and when the opponents scored yet again, he looked over at me and said, "I wish you would go back to work for a company. You are too smart to be out there hustling every day, begging strangers for money. Besides, think of your family. You could be earning a great income if you would just put that suit and tie back on."

But I couldn't do that. I knew who I was. I was an entrepreneur, a businessman – just like him. Dad was not so much concerned about my ability to build and grow a business. His intention was to help me understand that the business life is a tough life full of long hours, frustrations, stress and lost sleep. Since then, I have at times worked for companies and at other times had my own businesses, but the companies I worked for were always start-ups where I had the opportunity to do what I love on somebody else's dime.

Knowing who you are is the launch pad to owning your own business. An honest appraisal of your situation today – of your knowledge, of your skills, of your opportunities and of your weaknesses – will give you the knowledge necessary to be able to hear advice from those who love you, even when that advice does not match what you need in your soul. It is possible to hear what is said without fear of being lured away from the path you have chosen to travel, but that is very much dependent on you knowing your destination and knowing who you are today.

With those two simple pieces of information, we can create a plan to get you from here to there, a plan that will reduce risk and improve success. If you wish to revisit your answers, now may be a good time. There are no wrong or right answers, and certainly no judgements. This is just a way of identifying where you are today.

Remember that chart we drew during our destination discovery? Time to pull it out once more. This time, we will update it with a plot toward the bottom left hand corner. This plot represents where you are today. All we have to do now is join those two points and create the plan that will get us there. Sounds easy, right? Well, it really is. You have done the hardest part of this process. And while it seems to be all uphill from here, we are going to build steps with each step moving you forward to your destination.

A final thought: I hear lots of folk talk about identifying your strengths and weaknesses so that you can work on your weaknesses and eventually turn them into strengths. You may be surprised to hear that I totally disagree with that concept.

I believe that no amount of working on your weaknesses will turn them into strengths. Such a belief denies the fact that everybody has their own special set of skills. Taking an accountant who is lousy at plumbing and teaching him how to repair his pipes will result in nothing but more leaky pipes. Likewise, teaching a plumber to be an accountant will result in the IRS knocking down his door demanding payment for outstanding and unpaid taxes. Working on your weaknesses results in mediocrity at best – that is simply not good enough for the success we want to achieve.

That makes no sense to me. In my opinion, a better solution is to work on your strengths so that you can leverage that part of you to the greatest advantage and find a way to "fill your gaps" with people skilled in those areas.

So, if you are concerned that your answers to my questions simply show your weaknesses, don't be. This is what we are looking for. We want to figure out what we have to work with, what gaps need to be filled, and how best to leverage the skills and knowledge that you already have in order to prepare you for ownership of a business you can be proud of.

As is usually the case, the more effort you put into these foundational parts of the process, the greater your results and the easier the journey from here to your destination. Do you recall what I said about your inner self needing space to do its work? If you were totally honest with yourself in answering the questions, you will provide your inner self some guideposts. You are removing barriers and giving yourself space to grow, places and ideas to explore, and the beginning point to map your way to your destination.

To me, that is the most exciting thought. Can you believe that you have just given yourself permission to really move forward with this? I am sure that there are still plenty of fears and questions that are hanging around, disrupting your thought processes, and telling you that this is all impossible.

Embrace those thoughts, acknowledge their existence, and then tell them to get in the back seat – you are the one in control of this journey, not them. Remember my Kilimanjaro experience? It was not until the very hardest part of the journey that my inner voice decided to come on board with my journey. Sometimes, you just have to push forward through the doubts and fears until they decide to be your greatest cheerleaders.

So, what now?

It is time to celebrate – you know where you are going, and you know who you are. That deserves acknowledgement and celebration. Be good to yourself, reward the hard work you have put in, and know that from here the journey gets even more exciting!

# 6. Building Your Personal Blueprint

## Failure To Plan is Planning to Fail

This oft-repeated phrase, which I am sure you have heard many times, is true in all aspects of your life. From the time you were a child, people expected you to plan out your life. You know what they said – things like, "Get an education," or "Find a nice guy/girl, get married, have kids, build a career, buy a house, get old, and enjoy rocking chairs on the front porch until you die."

You are an entrepreneur, a budding business owner, a boss. Is that the life that your destination exercise envisioned for you? Or do you have something different driving you forward?

It doesn't matter why you are here, reading this book. Maybe your career has stagnated, maybe you need income, maybe your family expects you to own your own business, or maybe you just want to get rich? It doesn't matter why you are here. The only thing that matters is how you get from here to there, right? Right.

## Praying at the Gates of Mordor

The river was rapidly gaining speed as we rounded the bend. The sound of rushing water was getting louder but still far away. As I relaxed in the raft, looking at the blue sky with just a gathering of gray clouds, I marveled at the peace that can be found on the river. This was the seventh day that I had been floating the Chilco/Chilcotern/Fraser river system in British Columbia, Canada.

The river had a pace of its own; always moving forward, taking the raft wherever it wanted to take it. We had little control over nature...and the feeling was exhilarating. The freedom of following the path before us without thinking provided a sense of freedom that we, as humans, rarely feel. As we floated I understood that life is simple...we are the culprits that make existence hard.

I looked at the clouds. They were gathering quickly and getting very dark. In minutes, the sky was covered with heavy black clouds, fierce and threatening. Just then, we rounded the next bend in the river and saw it

.
The Gates of Mordor was a very apt name for this part of the river. Giant rock cliffs on both sides rose above us as the river narrowed to a seemingly impossibly narrow passage between the cliffs.

The first lightning bolt struck the ground a little way off the river to our right. The noise was deafening and thunderous, shaking the raft as we plunged toward the Gates. That was the first of many lightning bolts surrounding us as the storm unleashed its full fury. The smell of ozone filled the air. Hailstones the size of quarters pummeled us, and the river roiled in angry defiance to the unexpected storm that had caught us totally unprepared.

The raft kicked and bounced beneath our feet, bucking and jumping like a rodeo bull. One of the waves pushed us over the top of a large granite boulder that was sitting in the river and usually easy to navigate around. But not today.

Today we – myself, my wife, and our guide – found ourselves stuck atop the boulder. The skies thundered above us while the river screamed below. The hail continued to pound us. We were thankful that we had worn helmets this day on the river.

It has been said that time slows down when facing death. I can attest to that. In that moment, I had all the time in the world to reflect on what had brought me to this place, stuck on a rock in the middle of a raging river during a tumultuous storm. Me, a sixty-something-year-old finance guy who should have known better… What right did I have to think that I could handle the physical stress of rafting North America's most dangerous river?

It was about twelve months earlier that my (now) wife and I decided that we would do a whitewater rafting trip. I have a weakness for adventure and was quickly onboard when she suggested it. I pictured a lazy few days on a gentle river with a few rapids to shake us up. But no…as is usual with me, when I started looking into the options, I discovered the Chilco river. The adrenaline started pumping as I researched the White Mile (the longest continuous stretch of class 5 rapids in North America).

My destination was decided. I could see myself experiencing the rush of the water, the challenge of beating what so many had failed to do. (A movie called White Mile tells the true story of an ill-fated trip down the White Mile. Tragically, five or six of the party lost their lives that day.).

So, we decided to raft the Chilco and to raft it when the water was fastest and the rapids at their most dangerous. We decided to do a seven-day trip, where there was nothing but river, nature, the elements, and us.

We only had twelve months to prepare, and we needed a guide, someone who knew the river well. We started to plan. It was clear to us that we needed to prepare physically. We needed to build our strength so that our bodies could handle day after day of effort without succumbing to the aches and pains that are common to our ages. We developed a workout regime comprised of strength training, cardio, weightlifting, rowing, and everything else we could think of to build strength and stamina. We stuck to the plan – six days a week, even when we did not feel like it.

We knew we would need the right equipment including cold weather gear for the low temperatures and wool and silk for warmth when wet. We needed rain jackets, water shoes, neoprene gloves, and booties. We followed a list of suggested clothing needs and the instructions for packing in plastic bags and small totes.

As the date for departure got closer, we prepared ourselves emotionally and spiritually. There was no doubt that we were embarking on a possibly dangerous adventure.

We made sure that we were prepared in every way and as completely as possible.

And on that rock, in the middle of that storm, when our lives could easily have been at risk, what did I feel?

Fear? Nope.

Resignation? Definitely not!

I felt alive. My wife and I looked at each other, threw our hands in the air, punching holes in the hail as we laughed maniacally. It was one of the most exhilarating moments of my life.

You see, we had prepared, we had planned, and we had followed a process so that we were ready to deal with anything the river threw at us. We followed the advice of our guide to the letter. We did not try to change it, think we knew better, or even question why. When he said, "do something," we did it.

And when he said paddle hard, we threw ourselves over the front of the raft, pushing our paddles as deep and hard as we could, our toes barely clinging to the raft to keep us from falling out. The raft moved a little. Straining harder, the muscles in our backs pumped up and painful, we dislodged the raft and hurtled through the Gates of Mordor.

Within fifteen minutes of passing through the Gates, the sky cleared, the storm diminished, and the silence returned as we floated peacefully toward Big John, the final set of rapids on our journey. Big John lived up to its name and challenged us physically…but it was nothing like the Gates of Mordor.

When you plan, when you follow the process, when you follow the advice of those with more knowledge than you, then you are able to face the hurdles, the unexpected, and the seemingly impossible without fear, without worry, and with excitement.

And that is exactly what we are going to do now. We are going to create the process that you will follow to ensure you are able to get from here to your vision as quickly as possible, as painlessly as possible, and with more joy than you thought was possible.

## Creating Your Plan

Before we start on your plan, I want to take a few minutes to think about what we are trying to achieve here. Yes, I know we are creating a plan to get to your destination, but it is likely that your destination has more than one thing, right?

Perhaps a better way to think about your plan is to think in terms of it being the steps you need to take to be the entrepreneur who can get to the destination. Without a strong foundation, buildings collapse. Without a strong foundation, business owners fail.

What is the foundation that budding business owners need to have in order to be great business owners?

Let's ask that question another way.

What is it that people need in their lives to allow them to be happy, fulfilled, and living an abundant life with purpose? If you asked a hundred people, you would get a hundred different answers to this. But if you scratched a little deeper, you would find a trend. You would discover that most of the things those folk said could fall into just one of five different buckets. And you would see that all of those buckets are connected in some way.

The five buckets I see all the time are:-

- Financial stability

- Strong, healthy relationships

- Good health (physical and emotional)

- Career and education

- Passion and beliefs

Does it then make sense that to prepare for business ownership, to prepare for the opportunity to reach your destination, you must first build a strong foundation in each of these five areas?

Financial stability is a no-brainer, right? Anybody can see that financial stability can help you as you buy, build, grow or start a business. So, if that is the case and everybody sees it, why do so many folks try to do it without first getting a personal financial stability plan in place? That makes no sense to me. To take on the stress of a business when you are already stressed about finances is a recipe for disaster and failure.

What about healthy relationships? If you fight with your spouse today, what makes you think that will be any better when you have a business? Do you really think that your kids will magically see more of you when you own your own business? Let me tell you this truth. Unless you have a plan to get your relationships where you want *before* you become a business owner, you increase the risk of business failure dramatically. Now, another question. If you are not financially stable, how does that impact your relationships today? I can tell you that it adds stress and is one of the major causes of family relationship issues. Gain financial stability, and you will reduce stress and provide opportunity to work on relationships.

Health is another big one. Let's think through some logic here. Financial instability creates stress. Stress is bad for your health, both physically and emotionally. Poor health steals energy. Low energy reduces your ability to work your business, enjoy your relationships, and maintain financial stability. If your relationships suck, stress comes into your life and damages your ability to be efficient. It is all connected. Stress, insomnia, poor diet, lack of exercise, fear, insecurity – all these things spell failure to your business and will prevent you from reaching your destination.

Career and education. Get an education, they said. Get a job, build a career. I really don't care what they said. They are not you. You are here because you are ready to become the business person you always needed to be. A part of that is to know what skills you have learned in the past that will serve you in your new journey. Discard what no longer benefits you, without guilt. At the same time, there may be new skills or experience that you will need in order to be able to run your business the way you want to. The education you now need may be expensive and time consuming. Is that any reason to say it can't happen? Hell no! If you have financial stability, relationships on track, and health under control, you have actually found a way to make more of what you have. Now you are able to learn more of what you need. Simple, right?

And finally, we have passion and beliefs. There is nothing more tragic in my world than to find a client subjugating his passion and beliefs on the altar of the next dollar of profit. What you believe in is what drives your moral compass. To deny that belief, to act in a way that is opposite to your belief structure, to "bend the rules" a little here and there (surely that won't hurt) will indeed hurt. It will eventually lead you to confusion, guilt, lack of direction, and lack of joy. That is to be avoided at all cost. Do you know what may lead you to bend the rules? Financial instability and relationship stress are the two main reasons people lose their moral compass (along with greed in all its forms). As for your passion; you can satisfy that through hobbies or through your business. Nothing is more fulfilling than a business that does something you are passionate about. Your ability to enjoy that which gives you joy, that passion, is dependent on all the other areas of your life.

So, do you see how everything is interconnected. Everything impacts everything else. Your personal blueprint must create steps to prepare you in each of these areas, and that is exactly what we are going to do now.

## Your personal blueprint

I told you the whitewater rafting story for a very important reason. I want to encourage you to be open to something that is so simple that you may find it hard to believe it will work for you, especially in the place you are in right now.

As I prepared for my trip on the Chilco, I followed instructions. Even for "how" to pack a bag. Really? Having travelled around the world multiple times, through over a hundred and thirty countries, I was sure that I knew something about packing bags. Maybe I did, but I discovered that I knew nothing about packing for a whitewater rafting trip. I was willing to let go of my expectations and just do what I was told.

The end result? I had everything I needed, everything stayed dry, everything was easy to get to, and it all fit in one very small tote bag! Other passengers on the trip (in another raft) did not follow the instructions. Every day, they stressed about where things were, what got wet, what they didn't have – and it all fit in huge suitcases that were probably weighing over sixty pounds! It was a lesson for me: be willing to follow someone else's process sometimes because it is just possible that they may be right!

So, let's start your plan.

Pull out the chart that we have been working on. The first thing we are going to do is draw a line between the two points you have already charted. But it is not a straight line...it is a curved line. Now we are going to draw five boxes that form steps following the form of the curve we just drew.

OK. Good work. The most important thing we need to achieve to get you on the way to business ownership is to reduce stress. The biggest cause of stress in today's world is Financial Security. So, that will be the first box and the most important foundation for this transition toward business ownership.

The second box is Relationships. It is second because it will be much easier to work on this when a financial stability plan is in place. The third box is Health, and the fourth box is Career/Education. Then, the very top box is Beliefs/Passion.

Go ahead and write those descriptions in the boxes.

This simple chart is your personal blueprint for success. I know it seems simple (in fact, too simple) to work, but I ask that you let go of doubt and work with me here. The next couple of chapters will look at each of these areas and give you suggestions that will help you organize your plan in more detail.

Here is a little secret for you. The chart you just drew is your *secret weapon* to creating plans for your life or your business. The chart can be used for anything. For example: you have a business and want to create a new product, OK? You can build a chart that shows where you want to be and where you are today. Then, create the steps, which could be, for instance:

Identify customer
Identify problem
Identify solution
Test solution
Create product

Maybe you want to buy a house? Plot your two points. The boxes could be:

How much can I borrow
Financial fixes
Pre-approval
Find house
Make offer

Magic happens when we simplify our thinking. When we make the impossible into a series of small possible steps.

As you continue toward your journey of business ownership, you will find yourself in situations you did not expect; things do not happen the way you thought or wanted, or maybe the timing of things are all wrong. When you have a simple way of reducing the solution to small, bite-sized steps that allow you to remain on course with the big picture firmly entrenched, then your ability to enjoy the process is greater.

When you hit that rock at the Gates of Mordor, instead of praying for divine intervention, celebrate the fact that you are prepared for anything. Rocks in the river are only a temporary nuisance, not a dream-killing event.

Your blueprint to success is ready – now all you need is some guidance on how to use it, and that happens in the next few chapters!

*Have a question for me? Send me your ideas, comments, questions or complaints. I want to know what you think. You can reach me at:*
*www.IAmNotFinished.com/contact-us*

# 7. Create Financial Stability

## Money!

We all want it.

Most of us want or need more than we have. Some of us have exactly what we need while a small number have way more than they need. It is normal for us as human beings to feel pangs of jealousy for those who have more than they need. It is human for us to believe they should share what they have with those less fortunate. It is easy for us to find things to blame for us not having what we think we need. There is no more divisive thing in our society than the seeming gap between the rich and the poor.

Have you ever taken a moment to really think deeply about why "money" is such an important part of our life? We hear people say, "money makes the world go round" and "it is all because of the chase for the almighty dollar." But is that really true? In biblical terms, we are taught that "the *love* of money is the root of all evil." It does not teach us that money is evil, although many seem to have adopted that particular emphasis.

We have highly paid economists who advise the government on factors that affect the economy and the value of money. However, just like weather forecasters, they are often incorrect.

Everyone you talk to has a theory about how to make more money, or they are simply trying to hustle their way to what they need. I am about to share with you a theory, which, if you can accept it, will forever change the way you think about money and, in turn, the way you think about your coming business. Specifically, it will forever change how you think about your transition to financial stability.

## The Nature of Money

If you are anything like me, you have spent the majority of your life believing that money is "scarce." From when you were a child, when you were told that "mommy and daddy can't afford that new toy," you were being taught that money was scarce.

Then, you were taught that money was a reward for something that you have done. "Get a job, build a career, and you will earn good money" is the catch cry of my generation. The new generations are saying ,"I have a degree and two years' experience – I deserve more money." While both statements may be true, they infuse the wrong belief system in us. They connect your *effort* with a monetary *reward*. That is a mindset of scarcity; a mindset that does not believe that money is abundant. It is a mindset that stifles generosity and, quite frankly, is the cause of so much financial suffering today (and in the past).

Here is a better way to think about money: money is nothing more than a *reflection* of the value you, as a person, provides to the universe.

**It is not a reward, it is not earned, it is a reflection.**

Now, what is the definition of "value" within this context? That is quite simple...value is the impact you have to change people's lives for the better. The greater the change you can bring, the more people you can help, the more money flows your way.

This is not an economic discussion of supply and demand; it is a philosophical discussion of the nature of money. Since value (as defined) is limitless, the reflection of that value (being the flow of money) is also limitless. For evidence of this theory, look at Henry Ford, or Bill Gates, Zuckerburg, or the Google guys. What they did was to change many millions of people's lives. As a result, money flowed to them.

I know you are questioning the validity of this, perhaps asking about trust fund kids (I call them members of the lucky sperm club). Well, history has shown that unless they continue to add value to the universe, their wealth, their money, simply dwindles away. It flows away from them. The same thing with lottery winners. An astonishing 80% of big lottery winners are bankrupt within a decade.

So, if you can accept that money is simply a reflection of the value you add to the universe, then the next concept becomes easy to accept.

## Money is easy to get.

Just last week, I was talking to a young man who sought my assistance to define his business and clarify the steps needed to get there. When I explained this philosophy of money and then said that money is "easy to get," he immediately lit up with a huge grin and said, "Yes! All you have to do is add more value!"

As we move forward toward financial stability, it is important that we understand this simple philosophy even if it means you must "forget" those deep-seated ideas that well-meaning people have inadvertently filled your mind with.

To do that, there are a few simple things you can do to start the transition to the correct mindset:

### Tip 1: Do not buy lottery tickets.

Sure, it would be great to win the lottery. All your financial problems would be solved, and you could do whatever you want, right? But have you thought about what your subconscious is telling you when you walk into that store to buy a ticket? It is telling you that money is scarce and the only way you can get it is through luck. You are telling yourself that financial success is out of your control and is dependent on which little balls come out of a machine. Just stop… and start believing that your massive financial success is dependent on yourself and how much value you can add to the universe.

### Tip 2: Stop shopping at discount type stores like Walmart or Dollar Stores.

I do not say this because I don't want you to spend wisely but rather because of the mindset of the people who generally shop in those stores. They have the mindset that money is scarce and that they will struggle to keep food on the table. It is a mindset that will keep them in that exact lifestyle forever. Shopping in those stores allows some of that mindset to rub off on you. You will find it difficult to think in terms of abundance when all those around you live in scarcity. If you must shop there, be ready to pay the full bill of the person *behind* you when you go to the checkout. That act of generosity will help someone – adding to the value you contribute to the universe – and will keep you solidly in the abundance mindset. If you can't afford to do that, simply don't shop at a discount store.

### Tip 3: Never allow people to split a bill at a restaurant.

Never. If you cannot afford to pick up the tab for everyone, simply do not go. Splitting the bill allows for scarcity to enter your life. You then start to worry about who ate what, who drank what, etc. Splitting it 50/50 doesn't seem fair when some people had three beers and you only had a soda…get the idea? If you cannot afford to pick up the tab when someone suggests splitting the bill, do not go. Also, tip generously; this is not about the waiter's income, it is about the fact that they are there serving you, cleaning up your mess, and trying to add value to your life. It is now your turn to add value to theirs.

### Tip 4: Pick up a random stranger's bill at a restaurant.

This will add a great deal of value to that person's life. In fact, it could impact them in more ways than you could ever expect. I was at dinner one night with my son and his wife, and I noticed a young couple having what seemed to be a celebratory dinner. I asked my waitress to put their bill on my tab. When they discovered someone had covered their bill, the young lady burst into tears. It turns out this was their first wedding anniversary, and they nearly didn't go out because *both* of them had been fired that day.

Friends, if you are holding tight to the belief that money is scarce and resisting the mindset of abundance, you are preventing the opportunity to add value to people's lives. This is the backbone of gaining financial security. If we change the way we think about money, we change the way we use it.

**Big picture: Money is simply a reflection of the value we add to the universe. Money is easy to get. Just add more value.**

## Building Financial Security

We know that financial difficulties cause stress and impact every part of our lives. The stress can be so bad that you are unable to make any decisions. You will be scared that the decision you make will be the wrong one. Some folks simply give up and continue down the path to financial oblivion.

It doesn't have to be that way. While there is no magic pill that you can take to fix your finances, you can be on the path to financial stability in short order with a little planning, some deep thought and a willingness to take some difficult actions. That, my friend, will reduce stress and allow you to think more clearly about the business you will soon possess. After all, that is why you are here, right? To learn how to have your own business, whether to buy or build, and maybe even discover the right business for you?

I hope you have accepted that money is easy to acquire. If you don't believe me, just think about the gig economy (where people can earn a living by doing multiple "gigs". Sometimes it is called a "slash career" eg. Barista/uber driver/dog walker etc). It has never been easier to find income producing work if you are in need of quick cash. But that is not necessarily the right answer.

There is a law of nature that goes something like this: "Your spending will always increase to absorb every dollar that you have coming in." Here is a tough truth – you probably don't have an income problem; you probably have a spending problem.

Remember where happiness comes from? It comes from making more of what you have rather than wanting more of what you don't have. This is the fundamental truth that forms the foundation of how we are going to create financial stability in a very short time frame.

**Good Debt vs. Bad Debt**

The first thing we need to look at is debt and how much debt you carry. A very disturbing statistic in America is that something like 70% of the population are just two paychecks away from bankruptcy. That means that if you lost your job and could not replace it quickly, you will be in financial trouble, serious trouble. Why is this? Debt is the major culprit. Now, not all debt is bad, but when good debt and bad debt are combined, the result could be disastrous.

Good debt is debt that allows you a future benefit. For example, buying a house is generally considered good debt because the value of the house will increase at a faster rate than the interest on the mortgage over the term of the loan, under normal circumstances. Therefore, at some point in the future, you would expect to have an asset worth more than the amount of the loan against it.

Another form of good debt could be student debt by which you learn a skill that allows you to add value to the universe in future years. The last form of good debt could be a car loan in which the repayments do not add strain to your finances, and you need the vehicle to add value to the universe.

That is basically it! In general, good debt comes in just three varieties. Of course there are many ways that debt can be used to create wealth using advanced strategies, but that is far beyond the scope of this book, which simply seeks to answer questions of financial stability.

Bad debt, on the other hand, comes in many flavors:-

- Leasing a car
- Paying for a vacation on credit cards
- Buying a 90" flat screen TV on store financing
- Making minimum payments on your credit card
- Refinancing your home mortgage
- Using credit cards to buy something that you cannot afford to pay cash for

The first step to financial stability is to prevent any more bad debt from building up. We need to stabilize at your current level and not allow the problem to become worse. Now, I am quite a realist and understand that it is probably not possible or practical to simply stop using credit cards or store cards, so I have created a set of "rules" which will help you control bad debt:-

**Rule 1:** Never buy anything on credit if you do not expect to be able to pay it off in full within 30 days (the exception is absolute emergencies like medical needs, etc.).

**Rule 2:** Never allow your credit card and store card balances (combined) to exceed the balance in your savings account (clearly, if you have no savings, that cannot happen, but it is the objective).

**Rule 3:** Do not cancel credit cards when the balance becomes zero; lock it away somewhere safe, but do not close the account.

**Rule 4:** Use only one credit card. Pick the card with the lowest interest rate and use that.

**Rule 5:** Do not apply for any new credit cards or store cards (even when the banks are offering amazing deals).

These simple rules will start to get bad debt under control immediately and will allow you to start making progress toward financial stability.

## The Budget Myth

Most financial gurus will tell you that you need a budget.

They will tell you that you can find all sorts of cash savings if you draw up a budget and stick to it.

So, with all the right intentions, you dutifully draw up a budget. You painstakingly review every payment you have made for the last six months and list them on paper. You then examine each one and think about where you can make cuts and save some money.

When making a budget, you will say to yourself, "If I don't buy Starbucks on the way to work, I can save four dollars a day. If I turn all the lights off at 9 p.m. and sit in the dark, I can save fifteen dollars a month on the electric bill." And so on.

So, your take your new budget, and say let's not buy coffee on the way to work. (Of course, nobody has ever become wealthy by not buying coffee on the way to work, but the gurus seem to think that helps). You get up five minutes earlier in the morning to make coffee, and this works well for the first three days.

Then, the fourth day comes. Little Johnny forgot to wash his gym clothes and he has gym today, so instead of making coffee, you try to clean his gym clothes and make him kind of presentable. You stop for coffee at the Starbucks – it is only once – and tomorrow you will get back on budget.

But you don't!

These types of budgets *never* work because they are based on denial. The thinking is that if you are disciplined enough to deny yourself of something, then discipline will spread to other parts of your life. What a crock!

When you deny yourself because you are told you have to, you will fail. Just consider the number of times your diets have failed (because so many diets are based on denial) or your workout plans go astray (because they are based on denying something else so you can do that).

The truth is that budgets based on finding out what you can cut out on (deny yourself) have virtually zero chance of long term success. After all, who wants to have financial stability if they have to cut out Starbucks or their sports channel subscription?

Now, I am not suggesting you do not need to know where your money is going – in fact, the absolute opposite. You need to know exactly where the bulk of your money is going.

The budgeting process I'm going to teach you is what I call "The Bucket System." It is very easy to use and is based on the philosophy that you are the best person in the world to determine what you want to spend your money on. You will learn that you can have anything you want – it is simply a matter of priorities.

**Step 1:** List and total what you spend on the following every month
This includes:

- Mortgage payment (or rent)
- Electric, gas, water, trash
- Car payments
- Insurances (car, house, life, health, etc.)
- Student loan payments

Open a new bank account (this is the house bucket) and each pay period transfer enough to cover these payments to your new account. Most people can have this done by their employer who will pay that amount directly into that account for you, so you *never* see that cash. Then, set up payments from that account to ensure the payments are made on time every month. There will never be a problem meeting these bills again because the money is in the account already.

**Step 2:** List and total all your credit card and store card bills
The information you will need is:

- Balance
- Interest rate
- Minimum payment

Arrange the list so that the largest balance is at the top and the smallest at the bottom. Total the minimum payments so that you know how much you *must* pay every month. If you are the kind of person who has trouble being disciplined about paying your bills on time, you can set up another bank account (or bucket) and transfer the minimum payments directly from your pay so that the bills are automatically paid on time.

**Step 3:** Build a savings account and create a plan to reduce your debt

You have now deducted from your pay the minimum amounts needed to meet your financial obligations and have set up automated payment of those amounts. The two buckets you have set up have taken all the stress off you financially. You never need to worry about paying those bills again. Ever.

What is left is yours to do whatever you like with. However, the object is to reduce your financial stress long-term and get you in a financially stable position. (Don't have anything left? Then you have much bigger problems that will need more specialized assistance).

The first objective is to build a small savings account so that you would not be facing financial destruction in the event that you lose your job. The easiest way to do this is to determine the maximum amount you can save every month.

Commit to that amount and have it deducted from your pay and transferred to a savings account (another bucket). The objective is to build savings equal to at least three months of expenses.

That three months of cash must be in your savings account bucket before you change tactics. Once you have that, then we can go to your second objective.

The second objective is to create a plan you can live with to reduce your debt.

The easiest way to do this is to transfer the money that was going into savings into your credit bucket. Use that money every month to pay off the smallest balance first, then the next largest, and the next until you have paid off all your cards. You are not increasing balances because you are following the rules on credit cards, right?

When these "buckets" have been set up and are working as planned, you will know that everything is systemized.

There is no more guessing as to whether you can afford to go out to dinner or buy that new dress. All you have to do is look at the balance in your "living expenses" bucket and decide what your priorities are. You will soon learn that if you buy that dress, you may not have gas for your car. And you know credit cards are not going to be used, so you learn to make good decisions.

There is no need to deny yourself anything.

You just make the right decision for the moment based on where you want to spend your available money.

This is how I have lived for many years, and paying bills is never a problem. Systematic payment in a hands-off manner solves the stress that comes with financial life.

There are no decisions to make, no having to wonder how you are going to pay the rent – the money is always there, and the payment is always made.

This makes life simple.

## Additional Thoughts

The bucket system works in all situations, but if you find that your expenses are too high and there is not enough left over to feed yourself, some very difficult decisions will be required.

Here are two ideas for you to consider if that is your situation.

Generally, housing is the biggest expense you will have. As a rule of thumb, if the payments in your house bucket are more than 50% - 60% of your combined household income, you will have trouble staying in front. The simplest solution is to find less expensive housing. If you own your house, look into selling it and renting somewhere less expensive for a time. If renting, plan to move to a less expensive property.

Car expenses are an area where you could consider getting out of the repayment and purchasing a less expensive car.

These are the two easiest and fastest solutions to that problem. They are, of course, painful, but if you are in this situation, it is now time to fix it. A third option is to get more money, and as we have learned, money is easy to get – but I understand how difficult it is to have a mindset of abundance when every day is a struggle. Fix the struggle so that the abundant mindset can take you forward.

## Your Personal Blueprint

You can now build out your personal blueprint to financial stability. Everybody will create a different plan based on their individual personal situations.

You now have a plan to lead to financial stability.

Depending on where you are financially, you may need to spend some time creating that stability before you go into business for yourself. For some, it may just be a plan they can follow going forward, and if this is you, you are likely ready to move forward now. Whichever it is for you, this is perhaps the most important part of deciding whether to build or buy a business. It is certainly the key to business success or failure.

**Big picture:** the disciplines you have learned here are the exact methods and systems you will use in your business to ensure that you maintain control over spending and financial resources.

*Have a question for me? Send me your ideas, comments, questions or complaints. I want to know what you think. You can reach me at:*
*www.IAmNotFinished.com/contact-us*

# 8. It Is Not Just A Financial Decision

Owning your own business is one of the most exciting and purposeful things you can do as someone born with an inner entrepreneur. It is totally different to work for somebody else. Now, it is *you* who has to make all of the decisions in the business; it is you who has to decide what to pay employees, what products to offer, what marketing to do, how to manage your money…everything comes down to you.

Quite honestly, the combination of excitement and sheer volume of work can contribute to you becoming lost in your work. The hours can be long, the stress high. It becomes easy to forget the things that are most important to you.

It becomes easy to put aside non-business stuff for a time when you are less busy – and that time simply never comes. So, how do you maintain balance when you own your own business? What is the secret to managing all the other important parts of your life?

Well, it is really quite simple.

You start to create the disciplines required *before* you enter your own business. Listen. Everything is important and most parts of your life are a process… meaning there is no perfect ending. However, it is a process of steady improvement over time, which means having a plan, keeping to it, and managing all the parts of your life with balance.

We have already seen how to obtain and maintain financial stability. That is about 50% of the process to maintaining a balanced life. You will discover the other 50% in this chapter.

## Keeping strong relationships

While the first reason for business failure is mostly the financial stability of the owner, the second most predominate reason for failure is relationship breakdown. If you do not have a strong relationship with your partner, children, or family *before* entering business, it is unlikely that you will be able to improve them later. It is more likely that those relationships will fail, adding stress to you and reducing your ability to run your business.

**And then there is the unthinkable...**

Sometimes you say goodbye.

Not often, just sometimes.

If the diagnosis is plain, the prognosis clear, and the choices limited, there might be a time to say goodbye.

It must be a particular person with whom you share a bond, and then, maybe, there is a precious moment.

Then, sometimes, you say goodbye.

She was my wife for eleven years. She was also my best friend. I loved her. More than the beautiful love between husband and wife. The love of soldiers that have shared battle. The love of travelers who see the same world.

Husband and wife, who rejoice in life, expect and mourn suffering, would lose all for family, and believe in building on frank words.

Two people who cope with a wry smile, a bad joke, the occasional tear and the sweat of the brow.

Now, cancer ravages her body, and she will soon die.

Because she is the type of woman who knows that life will pass and can speak of a world thereafter; because I believe dying is a part of life and we can talk of it without folding, and because we are close, it is time to say goodbye.

Thank her for wonderful years together and the wisdom she has shared. Thank her for her teachings and support. Make sure she knows I am sorry to see her go.

Except, I cannot say goodbye.

I do not lack words, desire, or courage. I know exactly what to say.

I sit at her side, hold her hand, and look into her gentle face. Expression slack, baffled scowl, eyes adrift, she focuses on blank space. It is a shared moment, without sharing.

Does she understand my love, my loss, my pain? Perhaps she is already too far. The burden is on me to remember, to touch, to feel.

We sit quietly, her breathing shallow, disturbed only by an occasional cough; my breaths deep, disturbed by tightness in my throat.

We do not talk of family, sunrise, or sunset. No travel plans or food. No smiles or joy. No hope or dreams.

Two lovers share not goodbye, but silent moments at the end of life.

**Two days later**, my beloved Trish passed. I had gone away on business for a few days, and when I returned, I discovered she had not been well while I was gone. After several trips to various doctors, she was diagnosed with inoperative lung cancer.

Just six months later, she passed in my arms. If any of you have experienced this sort of loss, you will know that it is the greatest honor to be there comforting your loved one as they take their last breath…and it is the hardest thing you will ever do in your life.

People come into your life for a season. Sometimes a long one…sometimes shorter. They move on at exactly the right time. What I want you to understand here at a very, very deep level is that you must treat that relationship as the most important thing in your life while that person is a part of your life. Tomorrow may simply be too late.

Trish was not ready…she had much to do. Her time ran out…don't let yours.

**There are also people in your life who may be toxic to you.** Their negativity may be detrimental to you, creating self-doubt and trepidation as you move forward. There will be people who want to be helpful but give bad advice and others who really don't give a crap about you and just want what they can get. To be fully prepared for business ownership, you must be able to identify and discern one from the other and know what you want to do.

I have identified 5 different important relationships that you must be ready to work on.

**Relationship with a Spouse or Committed Partner**

This is the single most important relationship you will have today – or ever. This is the person who you love deeply; the one person in the world who understands you, can accept you as you are, and has promised to support you always.

Do not underestimate the value of this relationship.

Make sure you keep time for this person – quality time, not leftover time. Always be present when you are with her (or him). That means listening, sharing, talking, holding hands, etc. Leave the cell phone home when you go on a date. Do not keep cell phones or the TV in the bedroom. This is the most important relationship you have. Learn to nurture it today, and keep those habits in place when you start your business.

If you do not want your relationship, take the steps to end it before you go into business. Your business will simply complicate the entire process and cause added stress. Be honest with yourself and your partner.

**Relationships with Children**

Your children should be a major focus of your life.

They should not come before your partner because they will one day grow up and leave the nest. But they must remain a top priority for you.

When you become a business owner, you must ensure that you structure the business to allow you to attend school concerts, sports, and special times with your children. If you leave that up to your partner, resentment will eventually raise its ugly head.

And let me tell you this – when you are with your children, *be there.*

I cannot tell you how many times I watch fathers who have taken their son to soccer just to walk around the parking lot with their cell phones almost surgically implanted to their ears, while their son makes a great play or kicks a goal.

Really, guys?

Is that what you call having a relationship with your kids? I can tell you that time with your children is not at all lost time. Your children see the world differently than you. Talk with them, learn what they see – it will help you run your business better!

**Relationships with Extended Family**

Parents, in-laws, siblings, aunts, grandparents and cousins – what a group of complicated and sometimes difficult relationships to navigate.

I love families. I love the complexity and the differences.

But I don't love every family member. It took me quite some time to understand that just because they are family does not mean they have your best interests at heart. There is no law that states you must spend time with family.

I believe family is important, but those family members who are poisonous to my mindset, who bring negativity with them, or who are little more than leeches hoping to gain from my success do not get any of my attention. I waste no energy trying to help them. I waste no time trying to point out the error of their ways.

If I must see them at family gatherings, I remain polite but distant. That is the only way you can navigate family relationships and remain true to who you are.

Your task now is to identify who is who within your family and start the process of distancing yourself from the dream-killers.

## Relationships with Friends

It is often said that who you become is a composite of the five people you spend the most time with.

I 100% agree with that statement.

Your friends have the ability to lift you up or to bring you down. Loyalty is a two-edged sword. Loyalty to old friends who have your best interest at heart is desirable. Loyalty to friends who just want you to be like them, well, those are friends that you don't need.

The good news is that you can choose who you remain in contact with and who your friends are. This is 100% within your power. I urge that you choose well.

### Relationships with Co-workers, Colleagues, and Staff

These are very complex and not always dependent on you. You are not responsible for how these people feel or what they do.

You are, however, responsible for how you treat them. Remember the nature of money? Treat you co-workers and staff fairly and consistently. Do a little more, and you start adding value to their lives. Help them succeed before you seek your own success.

Now, you can draw your relationship blueprint. Everybody will have a different one depending on what difficulties they have.

## Health

There is nothing like owning your own business to destroy your health. If you do not have healthy habits prior to being in business, it is unlikely that you will start afterwards.

The biggest problem with owning your own business is the temptation to work long hours and try to do it all yourself.

I understand why this temptation is there. You hear from lots of successful start-ups that it is all about the hustle. I can tell you horror stories about how many hours I thought I had to work when I started my first business. It's easy to see how Gary V. makes a grand living by posting on social media about how much hustle he has going, flitting from one airport to another, going from meeting to meeting – just making it happen!

Let me tell you this: there is nothing romantic about having dinner in London and lunch the next day in Paris. Every four star hotel in the world looks exactly the same, regardless of which city or country you happen to be in. Sitting in airports working on your laptop is the most inefficient business activity you can find.

Some years ago, I was working with a client who wanted me to help him raise capital for his business. One look at his business plan told me that the business would never work. I worked with him, and we identified an entirely new business that we both believed would work.

We wrote the business plan in a few days, tested the idea with some trusted experts, refined the plan, and then started to raise capital. That, in itself, is unusual because to raise capital without at least a prototype product and some revenue traction is very rare.

In this case, the product idea was strong enough that we were able to raise significant seed capital and set out to start building a minimal product.

Then, we ran into problems.

You see, Rick was convinced that unless he did everything himself, unless he micromanaged his team, unless he spent twenty hours a day and seven days a week on his business, it would fail.

The result?

Within a few weeks, he was burnt out.

In less than three months, he had burned through all the seed capital and was forced to close the business. No prototype was built. His employees were laid off, and he found himself with no job, no business, no friends…and barely keeping his family together.

Rick was suffering from what I call "business delusion syndrome" – a malady that business owners catch the day they get their own business. The symptoms include:

- Exceedingly long hours
- Insufficient sleep
- No exercise
- Poor diet
- Chemical assistance
- Poor decision-making skills
- Anger
- Depression
- Indecisiveness

Any one of these symptoms will have a negative impact on your business, your relationships, your finances, and your emotional and physical health. So, what do you do about it?

There are a few things that can be done *before* you start your business, and a couple that will happen as you start working it.

**Tip 1: Make a pact with yourself**

Perhaps a written contract that you will only work on average "X" hours per week in the first year and "Y" hours per week after that. I have found most business owners can work less than sixty hours in the first year, and less than fifty hours after that if they decide that is what they want to do.

**Tip 2: Start eating a balanced diet today.**

Do *not* go to the extreme of denying yourself the things you love to eat. Just become aware of what you are eating and how often. If you are currently significantly over or under a healthy weight, get some assistance to get your body closer to where it should be.

**Tip 3: Change your lifestyle so that you get at least seven (but ideally eight) hours of sleep a night.**

Any less than that and your brain and body do not have an opportunity to fully regenerate, and you will experience low energy, tiredness, and mental fatigue.

**Tip 4: Start an exercise regime.**

I am not suggesting you become a gym rat or engage in anything extreme. I make a habit of exercising for at least thirty minutes, often an hour, for five or six days a week. I have a home gym set up that allows me to do strength training and cardio work.

I like the mornings because it gets my body moving and the blood circulating. I find my day is balanced emotionally and my mind far more creative when I exercise in the morning. An added bonus for us early starters is the knowledge that we have already got a head start on the day and can watch the world awaken long after we have already started.

This psychological benefit is, to me, the secret to emotional balance and stress-free work days. I know some people claim to work best at night and that their rhythms support that. OK. So still exercise before you start your day, OK?

**Tip 5: Reduce reliance on chemicals.**

Alcohol, drugs, cigarettes are all bad for your physical and emotional health. I have no problem with enjoyment of these, but do not allow them to become the crutch that allows you to sleep or the escape from your problems. Sleep comes from solving challenges, not from running from them.

**Tip 6: Fill your gaps!**

When you have your business, an honest assessment of your skills and knowledge will tell you what "gaps" you need to fill. Employ the best people to fill those gaps, and then let them do their jobs.

I cannot stress enough how you must take care of your health if you want to own a business. Your business depends on it, your family depends on it. Now, you can build out your health blueprint.

## Career and Education

Some folk go into their own business with the necessary skills to run it well from day one. These are mostly people who have been planning it for some time and have consciously planned their career and education in a way that gives them the skills needed to be able to operate their business.

But what if you haven't done that?

What if you are an engineer who wants to open your own engineering consulting firm? Do you have the skills to know how to market, how to get more customers? Do you know the legal requirements? Are there any regulatory compliance issues you have to understand? Do you need any special licenses? Or insurance? What about labor laws? Taxation laws? Business structure?

Even if you are an expert in the product or service that your business will offer, there is a great deal more that you will need to understand before you are ready to operate your own business.

The time to discover what you need to know and learn it is before you actually start.

Your knowledge "gaps" can often be filled by employees that have those skills, but I highly recommend you learn some basics in the following areas:

- Marketing
- Sales
- Human resources
- Accounting
- Taxation
- Contract law

I am not suggesting you need to go back to college and do a four-year degree in accounting before you start, but I do recommend that you do some research, read some books, and get a good fundamental knowledge of these areas. There are three main reasons for this:

1. You can then interview potential employees well and understand whether they have the knowledge to actually do the work you need done

2. You can check their output and know whether they are doing well or just bluffing

3. You can keep track of your business; you must be able to rely on your team to do their jobs, but at the end of the day, *you* are the business owner who must understand every aspect of your business

Take an inventory of your skills, knowledge and aptitude.

Build out your personal education blueprint now. Make sure to include your own skill needs.

## Passion and Beliefs

This is all about what *you* believe and what *you* are passionate about. In other words, this section is about you and only you. It does not matter what you partner thinks, nor your children, nor your parents. Not even your pastor or religious advisor.

**This is about you.**

Let's start with *passions*.

Most people have things they are passionate about. For some, it is hobbies. I have a 1973 Mustang Convertible in running order but in need of some restoration. Some people would be passionate about the restoration project and spend all their spare time doing a perfect job. Me? Not so much. I am more interested in keeping it in working order so that I can enjoy a sunny Sunday drive. Other people are passionate about causes, like no-kill dog shelters, global warming, or politics.

When thinking about your business, it is always a good idea to have a business that is involved in some way with what you are passionate about. It may be directly or indirectly related. It may simply be that you can use your business to fund your passion.

Owning a business is not always easy. And the closer the business is related to something you are passionate about, the less it will seem like work when you are running it. Your passions will help you get through the darker times when you feel like giving up, and they will energize your thoughts and creativity and will help you feel like you are doing something good.

Your *beliefs* are perhaps even more important than your passion.

Sometimes, the two can be the same, but often they are a little different. Most people find their best selves when they believe in something bigger than themselves. That could be their faith, it could be nature, or it could be called the universe or God.

It could be a cause that has touched them deeply. It is usually something external to them, something that has the ability to support a belief system. This belief system in turn can control the moral compass that we each live by.

That moral compass is what must be at the foundation of every business decision you make, every interaction with a customer, supplier or employee. Your moral compass must always be the guide that allows you to know what you should do in any situation.

Once we start discussing beliefs and passion, we have come almost full circle to where you are today. You need an honest appraisal of who you are, as well as where you are. And you need to commit to maintain the characteristics of that person even as you become the person in your destination.

The personal blueprint for your Beliefs and Passion will be very personal to you. It will be the result of some deep searching to understand who you are and will serve as a stake in the ground as you transform to entrepreneur. That stake in the ground is to keep you fully grounded, to remind you of what is important to you, and to symbolize what you want to retain – no matter what happens as you grow your business.

This is the blueprint that will reduce the risk of you becoming someone you don't want to be. It will keep you in touch with reality.

*Transforming from ordinary person to extraordinary entrepreneur is a hazardous journey that impacts every part of your life. Have a question for me? Send me your ideas, comments, questions or complaints. I want to know what you think. You can reach me at:*
*www.IAmNotFinished.com/contact-us*

# 9. Do You Buy It – Or Build It?

Well done!

You have done a lot of the heavy lifting to get to this point, and you will be using that work to guide you as you make perhaps the biggest decision of your career.

At this time, I would like you to go back and revisit the work you did on your destination. Have your thoughts changed at all? Has the destination become clearer? Are there additional aspects you would like to include in the vision of your destination?

Now would be a great time to go back and make any changes you need. It is that vision of your destination that will be a foundation for the decision of whether to build a business from scratch or whether to buy an existing business.

## What Business Type Gets You to Where You Want to Go?

Using your destination as a guide, we will look at what sort of business you really want. I see businesses as falling within three main types:

Type 1: A business that sells a single product, or group of products of a similar nature, to a market with similar tastes or needs; examples of this could be a retail clothing store, a carpet cleaning business, or a fitness franchise

Type 2: A business that develops and sells multiple products/services into different markets, with each product/service designed for the needs of the specific market it is intended for; an example of this is a software development house, furniture manufacturer, or perhaps an engineering consulting firm

Type 3: A business that has moved beyond merely a business and has become what I call a *movement*; this type of business has developed such a rapport with its users that they have become fans and will not buy similar products from anybody else

To better understand the differences and the relative appeal of each type of business, let's look at three tech giants of the 80's and 90's.

**Palm Pilot** was the first company to make a commercial success of portable electronic notepads that could be synced to your PC and allow for contact lists and memos to be fully portable. It was a huge success and realized massive valuations when it went public. Unfortunately, it was really just a product. There was no business built around the product other than newer, slightly better versions of the product. Eventually, the smart phone came along and changed it all. Palm Pilot could not compete, lost market share, and eventually died a slow and painful death for its stockholders. Single product businesses are very much subject to the whims and fashions of the times and can lose market virtually overnight when something newer comes along – and it always does eventually.

**Contrast that with Microsoft**. Microsoft took the approach that it was going to have its software on every desk top computer in the world. The introduction of the PC gave Microsoft huge opportunities, but it did not stop with just operating systems. It built search engines and enterprise software; it created server software and a complete suite of products that made using computers more intuitive and easier. Microsoft is the software giant it is today because it built a real business that changed and grew with its market and the changing characteristics of the marketplace. Microsoft is clearly in the second category of businesses.

**Finally, we have Apple.** By no means did Apple have an easy path to success. Tumultuous leadership changes, wrong products, high costs, and poor initial quality nearly doomed Apple to the annals of history, a fate that would make it interesting only to people wanting to learn what *not* to do. But then, Steve Jobs introduced the iPod, and everything changed. Apple disrupted industries.

I am not prepared to state that only Apple could build products that nobody else could build. While some may disagree with me, I believe that many of the competing hardware manufacturers would have been able to make equally good products.

So, why did Apple explode while others languished? You could argue that they were first to market, and that could certainly be an advantage. However, I believe the reason is that Apple understood its customer base better than anyone else. It knew that its customers wanted both style and functionality.

And by providing what they wanted, Apple built a fan base of people who are Apple crazy. **They created a movement.** The most powerful of the three business classes.

Now, I know you are not looking at necessarily becoming the next Apple or Microsoft…but maybe you are? In either case, the first decision you need to make when you look at your destination is this: which of these three business categories is going to achieve my destination?

Which type will get me exactly where I want to be?

**What product is right for you?**

There are so many product choices that sometimes this decision is nearly impossible.

After all, how do you know if you want to sell physical products or digital products? Do you want to retail or wholesale? Do you want to sell business to business (B2B) or business to consumer (B2C)? If B2B, do you want to sell to small businesses or create enterprise solutions? Do you want to do consulting type work? If so, how do you find clients?

The questions are virtually endless, but you have in your hands three pieces of information that will guide you along this difficult path.

You have the work you did on your destination; you have the work you did on your passions and beliefs, and you have the work you did on career and education. These will be your guiding light to answering the above questions.

Why do I say this? Simple.

**Because success is always found at the intersection of what you love doing, what you are good at doing, and market opportunity.**

That little area where all three circles collide is the secret to your success as a businessperson, financially, and personally. This small area is what you need to find before you can decide whether to buy or build your business. Let's dissect this thought a little to try to understand why this is so important.

## What You Love Doing

Look back at the work you did on your passion and beliefs.

Your passions are what you love doing. They are what will keep you pushing forward when things get tough. They will not let you give up. They are such a part of the real you, the inner you, that to let go of them would be physically painful.

It is often said that if you love what you do, you will never work a day in your life. I find this to be true. I am passionate about business, about creating opportunities for personal success through business, and now I am passionate about helping others find their way into business. My work is a joy to me, never a burden.

When what you love is part of your business, work becomes a joy that you look forward to every day.

## What You are Good at Doing

OK, so we are not all blessed with an incredible ability to be great at everything we do.

I love fine dining and am quite passionate about great food and wine. It is a guilty pleasure that I sometimes enjoy far too frequently. I love the restaurant industry. I sit at a table and my mind automatically starts to calculate how many seats there are, how often the tables turn, what the average sale is, and so on. I can't help but think about how the restaurant could function more efficiently.

I could never own a restaurant. I would love to – it would feed one of my passions – but I know nothing about food preparation, the cooking process, or the back-office operations. That is not my thing, and although I could learn it, I know I will never be great at it.

When you are good at something, you know it intimately. You know how it works, how to improve it, how to do it right. You can fix it with your eyes closed and know something is going to break before it breaks.

That is what I mean by "what you are good at doing."

If you can find where that meets what you love doing, you are most of the way to identifying where success can be found. And you already know what you are good at – it is in your career and education worksheets.

**Market Opportunity**

This is the most important of the three elements we are looking at now. Market opportunity can be found where a few simple things are present.

1. You can identify a problem that you have or an identifiable customer actually has. This cannot be some vague thing like "people need more exercise." It must be specific and a real problem like: "executives over the age of forty-five need more strength training to avoid osteoporosis in later life." The problem also needs to have an element of urgency that will get customers buying today.

2. You must have a solution to the problem. That solution must be able to be described in a way that your user will *want* to buy it. In our example, the solution could be, "our new strength training course will keep you fit and in good health. Clinical tests show that people completing our training have reduced the risk of osteoporosis by over 40%." That is a solution that people will buy.

3. Your target customer must have available cash to spend or have access to cash to spend on your product. Competitors in the marketplace validate the existence of the market, but an oversaturation may become too competitive.

4. Your product should never be seen as a commodity. For example, if you are in a consulting position, you must be capable of being value priced and not charged by the hour. If a physical product, it must be able to be portrayed as a premium product or, better yet, start of a movement.

5. You must know how to reach your customers, where they hang out, what they like to do, what they already spend money on.

If all these things are present, you may have market opportunity for your product (but you will never know for certain until you start to sell it).

The decision on whether to buy or build is becoming easier now as you know where success can be found, you have an idea of the product you wish to sell, and you know what type of business you want to have.

**Should I Buy or Build?**

The work you have just done on identifying where success can be found is the driving factor in this question. However, it would be remiss of me to not discuss the options that are available, and which are likely to be best in each situation.

There are basically four ways you can become a business owner (regardless of whether that is by yourself or in partnership with others):

1. Buy an existing independent business that offers product/services that "fit" with the solution you discovered in "market opportunity"

2. Buy an existing franchise business that offers the solution you have

3. Start your own business from scratch

4. Buy a new franchise that offers the solution you want to sell

Each of these options have pros and cons which we will look at now.

**Buying an Existing Independent Business That Offers Products That Fit with Your Solution**
**Pros:**

- The existing customer base provides opportunity for immediate revenue flow
- The existing customer base may validate the existence of your market opportunity

- The existing customer base allows for inexpensive market research for new product development
- The existing business may provide opportunities for finance by leveraging assets and existing cash flow
- The current owners may be willing to stay on during a handover period – reducing risk of "getting it wrong"
- There is likely to be an existing infrastructure – employees, marketing, legal, accounting, tax, etc.

**Cons:**

- Initial purchase price will absorb cash that could be used for other purposes
- Existing customer base may not remain loyal
- Assets may not be in good condition and will need replacing requiring more funds
- Interest on financing will eat into profit and cash flow
- Existing staff may be reluctant to embrace new ownership ideas
- Existing staff may leave

**Buying an existing business** is a good proposition for people who:
a) Have some available cash
b) Have decided their preferred business type is the first type (a business selling goods or services of a similar nature to customers with similar likes/needs)
c) Have identified their market opportunity as something that fits within the product group of the existing business
d) Are looking for a "lower risk" entry into business ownership
e) Lack the skills and knowledge necessary to build out a team of advisors quickly

**Buying an Existing Franchise**

**Pros:**

- Good records of past performance reduces risk of unknowns
- Strong support from franchisor
- Marketing concepts prepared at franchisor level
- Product development at franchisor level
- Systems and procedures in place and well documented
- Likelihood of continued customer loyalty after ownership change
- Relatively easy to obtain finance

**Cons:**

- No control over new products
- No control over marketing/advertising
- Must follow set procedures
- Franchise fees continue in form of royalties, advertising costs, and equipment/supplies purchasing
- Limited capability to create operational efficiencies outside of pre-designed systems and procedures

**Buying an existing franchise** has some great benefits and is most suitable for people who:

a) Have some available cash
b) Want to own a business but not necessarily work in it (absentee ownership)
c) Do not want to create their own products
d) Do not know where their market opportunity is, but still want a good business

e) Want to be in business for themselves but not by themselves (the franchisor will work to help them succeed)
f) Have identified their market opportunity as something that fits within the product group of the existing business
g) Are looking for a "lower risk" entry into business ownership
h) Lack the skills and knowledge necessary to build out a team of advisors quickly

**Start Your Own Business from Scratch**

**Pros:**

- No restrictions on products/markets/style of business
- No existing customers or culture to be concerned about
- Can create the business operations and processes in accordance with own beliefs
- Can start part-time and grow as profits occur
- Can pivot if products need to be changed/adapted or scrapped
- Does not use cash in acquisition costs
- No legacy problems from previous owners/staff/systems, etc.

**Cons:**

- Very difficult to get funding until product demand is proven and traction is gained
- No validated market
-  path to follow
- Need to build infrastructure, systems, procedures, team as business grows
- Risk of failure

- Longer time to cash flow

**Starting your own business from scratch** is usually the right solution for people who:

a) Have limited finances and are willing to build over time as customers are found
b) Have some basic business knowledge or are willing to learn as they go
c) Have a very clear idea of their product, the problem they are solving, and how to connect with their customers
d) Want to build a business serving multiple different markets/customers with a plan to become a movement
e) Knows or can learn how to build out a team that "fills the gaps"
f) Is willing to change directions if his product fails to get market validation
g) Has a deep burning desire to do it himself!

**Buy a New Franchise**

**Pros:**

- Get the benefit of being in business while also having franchisor support
- Instant products that have been tested with market validation
- Site selection and build out assistance from franchisor
- Market research; demographics studies reduce risk of failure
- Systems and procedures for efficient operation well-documented and tested
- May be possible to obtain some acquisition funding from finance sources

- May be able to acquire multiple site licenses
- Get to build it from scratch with experienced support team

**Cons:**

- Initial franchise fee and ongoing fees will eat capital
- No control over product, marketing, advertising etc
- No control over systems/procedures
- Risk of failure nearly as high as a non-franchise start-up
- Poorly performing franchises can often be taken back by franchisor

Buying a new franchise carries most of the same issues as buying an existing franchise with a couple of major differences:

- When buying a new franchise, the rewards for success can be significantly higher than when buying an existing franchise. This is because the new franchise owner gets all the benefit of taking the initial risk and building the business. The second owner "pays" for that benefit when buying an existing franchise.

- The risk of failure is higher for a new franchise. An existing franchise has a validated history of performance. A new franchise is an unknown quantity.

**Buying a new franchise** is suitable for the same people who purchase an existing franchise with two exceptions:

a) They must be willing to accept greater risk
b) They must be willing to work in the business until it is well-established.

## Do You Now Know Whether You Want to Build or Buy?

As a final thought, this decision does not have to be set in concrete today. You may be thinking that buying is right for you, and when the search begins for the right business, you can't find it or can't find it at a price that makes sense. You then may have to think about building it.

Take your time working through this process. Your success in future business ownership will be determined largely by making the right decision at this stage of the process. It is worth your time to avoid a costly mistake.

*Have a question for me? Send me your ideas, comments, questions or complaints. I want to know what you think. You can reach me at:*
*www.IAmNotFinished.com/contact-us*

# 10. The Search Begins

## What next?

Really, it is the perfect time to take care of business – to put all your fears aside, to cast any self-doubt to the winds, and to start on your journey of business ownership.

You can do this!

You have done the hard work, and now know what your path is. Not only do you know whether you want to buy a business that you can run, but you know what your product/service is and what type of business you want to have. You know where you want to go and what steps to take to get there.

You could not be better prepared to become a business owner than you are today.

That preparedness puts you years ahead of the many people who think about business ownership or maybe even want business ownership but never take the first step toward it. You are also years ahead of those people who just jump in to a business without giving it much thought. They risk their financial health, physical and emotional health, family, and more – simply because they did not think first.

I was reading an article just today that was looking at the failure rate of businesses started by millennials – it is over 90%. The reason given for most of those failures? That the product was not a match to the market needs!

You know that will not be your problem because you have done the work to identify the problem and the solution. You will, of course, have to validate that your solution is the best one for the problem, but that comes as you enter business ownership.

You are smart enough to change your product to fit the market as you work through the validation process. You are financially stable or working toward that point. You know what needs to be done, and you know how to do it. You know your strengths and the gaps you need to fill. You have aligned your passions and beliefs with your product and business type.

So now you are ready. Before we go further, there is one more valuable piece of information that you really need to understand, to grasp with both hands, and to never let go.

The greatest opportunities are found where there is risk.

If you are the kind of person who wants to watch and learn from others' mistakes, you will find yourself encountering a significant obstacle along the way: by the time you enter the fray, the opportunity has diminished because the risk has diminished.

I understand the need to mitigate risk as much as possible and applaud that desire, but I also counsel balance.

**The absence of risk equals the absence of opportunity.**

With what you know today, you have mitigated a great deal of the risk associated with business ownership. It is now the best time in your life to take a deep breath, step outside of your comfort zone, and start doing. It is time to start searching for the perfect business to buy, or to start building your own, depending on which course you have determined is right for you.

But there are a few things to consider with both of these options.

### Buying an Existing Business

Buying an existing business can be simplified into an easy-to-follow process that can help you identify a great business and make the lowest possible offer with the best chance of success. This does not come down to luck – it comes down to knowing what you are doing.

First, you must decide whether you want the business to be local to you, or whether you are willing to travel or even relocate. Opening a wider geographical area will provide greater opportunity to find the right business.

After you have identified your product, create a list of the type of businesses that would work with the product you wish to sell. There are literally hundreds of thousands of businesses for sale in the US alone every day, but only a small percentage will be what you are looking for. You need to narrow down your search quickly.

You can find businesses to buy through literally thousands of business brokers. I recommend you use these brokers to practice your skills, learn how to value a business, and learn what questions to ask. I strongly suggest you *do not* buy your business through one of these brokers (that is unless you are happy to pay 20% to 30% more for the business than you need to).

Business brokers serve a valuable purpose. They bring buyers and sellers together, but they are working to get the highest price possible for the business. They have often "bought" the listing in the first place by persuading the seller that they can get a much higher price because of their client list, their presentation, their blah blah blah. The hapless seller loves the idea of how much his business is worth and signs up with the broker even though the broker will get 10% - 20% of the eventual selling price.

The broker now has a problem. He has to attract buyers willing to pay a higher price for his clients business. How does he do this? Really, quite simply – he presents financial information after taking out all the payments made to the owner or his family. He then calculates the cash flow to owner and talks about that, which can be significantly different to the accounting (or real) profits or losses. A really good broker can take a loss-making business and show it as producing cash flow to the owner.

These little tricks, while not outright lies, tend to make the business look far stronger than it actually is, and therefore the hapless buyer agrees to pay more than he should.

This is the major reason I say that you should use business brokers to help you hone your skills when assessing businesses but not to buy through them. Also, the seller pays the broker fees from the proceeds of sale. If you can find your business before it goes to a broker, your cost is instantly reduced by at least 10% and, very often, much more.

The best deals can be found in two ways:

**Option 1:** You can search through the few websites that list businesses for sale by owners. These sites charge a listing fee to the seller but usually do not take a commission of the sales price. This generally means a slightly lower asking price.

**Option 2:** Look for businesses in the areas you want to be located in that fit your "right business" description. They probably do not have "for sale" signs and often the owner has not even thought of selling. Having created your list, simply go and visit the business. Ask about the owner and speak to them if you can. Tell them that you are looking for a business to buy – ask them if they know of anybody that may be interested in selling. Do not tell them you want to buy their business. Just start the discussion and leave contact details so they can connect with you if they think of someone.

Be patient and do this as many times as you can, but never tell the owners you are interested in their business. At some point, you *will* get that lead you are searching for, and then the real game begins. When you make contact with the owner of a business who you *know* is interested in selling, you simply have a conversation to try to understand why they are interested in selling. In most cases, these people are wanting to retire and need a way to cash out, but they also want to leave a legacy – their life's work is important to them, and they don't want a stranger taking over and changing it.

Boom!

This is the seller who will sell to someone they believe will look after their "baby." Their interest is not so much in maximizing money but rather that they believe you will carry their family tradition forward. This is the seller that is likely to carry a portion of the note at low interest rates just to make it possible for *you* to buy.

As you build a relationship, they will start to trust you and eventually will do anything to get you to take their businesses.

I have heard of several people who have taken this approach, and the owners have literally given the business to them with the assurance that payment will be made after three years. In one case, the owners just handed over the keys of a significant business…free.

Yeah…it works.

Of course, these are extreme examples but show what can be done by forging these relationships.

Finding the right business to buy should not be rushed. It should be systematic; it should follow a process. With practice the negotiations will become easier, and you will find better solutions to fund the purchase.

With patience, you *can* and *will* find the perfect business to buy at the right price.

**Build Your Own Business**

Building your own business is certainly not easy and carries a significant amount of risk (which, as we know, is where great opportunity can be found). To mitigate that risk, you will need to build a team of advisors who can help you navigate through the myriad start-up land mines that can derail you before you start.

Initially, you will need someone with legal skills, accounting skills, and bookkeeping skills. It is possible that you may find this at your local CPA office or through some of the hourly labor websites like guru.com. It is important before you start your business that you get great advice on the legal structure and tax implications.

Failure to set up in the best way will cause you problems very quickly and may cost you a ton of money. You will also need a banking relationship, and a good insurance agent. With these skills, available, you will be in a strong position to start your business.

As I said earlier, the number one reason for business failure is failing to procure product/market acceptance. You have already mitigated this risk significantly with your work on product development. In my opinion, the biggest risk to all entrepreneurs (and that means *you)* is failure to remember the one rule of entrepreneurship...

## You Must Still be Alive at the End of Today!

This means specifically that every decision you make and every action you take must be directed toward the objective of still being in business at the end of the day.

The temptation for most people who start their own business is to get a product built – but not just any product... the perfect product, the perfect solution.

Even when they understand that they should be creating a minimum viable product, they have a tendency to want to create a product that is far more than minimal. So they start to build a Ford when they should be building a pedal car.

They end up trying to build a Ferrari when even the Ford would have been overkill. Guess what happens? The Ferrari never gets built, the problem never gets solved, and the entrepreneur goes broke.

The saddest part?

An idea that could have changed people's lives and could have added value to the universe has not been birthed. And where does the money go? Away! It goes to someone who adds value to the universe.

So, what does this mean to the process of starting your business?

It simply means that you need to be careful to keep your ego in check. As quickly and cheaply as you can, start by validating that your product idea matches the market need.

If it doesn't, refine or change it.

In the business world, this is called a *pivot*. Do not fall into the trap of loving your ideas so much that you think everybody else must also love them. They won't. Be willing and prepared to kill your own ideas and challenge your own expectations.

Grow s-l-o-w-l-y.

Do not overextend your resources, especially your own time/effort/energy. Hustle is a good quality, but hustle that takes your eyes off the ball (the objective to survive to the end of the day) can be deadly to your business.

So, in summary, find your team, validate your product, create your minimum viable product, test it, and get some sales/traction. Grow slowly, keeping your eyes firmly on the destination, but stay alive at the end of each day.

Success will find you because you have done all the hard work already.

### How to grow a real business?

There is a very basic business plan that your product development efforts should follow.

The steps are simple.

Start with a low cost or free product to be used as a lead magnet. Some portion of the people who get that product will purchase your next, more expensive product. Some portion of them will buy your expensive product, and some portion of them will buy your top-end product.

It is an order of magnitude simpler to sell another product to an existing customer than it is to find a new customer.

As you think about growing your business (whether you have bought it or built it), this product development plan should be the guide for your thinking.

### Life is Simple

As humans, we have a tendency to make things far more difficult than they need to be. I have shown you how to simplify complex thought processes into easy-to-use steps to own or buy your business. Check out from time to time, get back to your true essence, and discover the simplicity of life. It will energize you and nudge your creativity to the surface.

## Last September ....

Are you aware of the time?" Laura asked gently as I examined the stubble on my chin. Neglecting to shave for a few days sure did make me look older, almost like every picture I had seen on wanted posters!

I quickly made the decision to shave, even though we were on somewhat of a deadline, and time marches on regardless of whether we want it to, or not.

I looked at the clock on the wall....8:45 a.m. We still have time.

We had spent the night in a gorgeous little bed and breakfast, tucked away in a back street of Mission Beach. The room was Victorian in design but large with a comfortable king size bed and a sitting area. The bathroom belied the Victorian style – modern and with all the best facilities.

We were both excited for the planned activities of the day, while the aroma of bacon, eggs, toast and coffee beckoned us. Breakfast was a sumptuous affair with fresh fruit (pineapple, banana, passion fruit and more), which seduced our taste buds as we enjoyed the solitude and peace.

A solitude that was soon broken with the arrival of other houseguests, an Italian traveler with her French husband. Over bacon and eggs, we engaged in the typical sort of small talk that fellow travelers indulge in whilst on the road.

"Where have you been?"

"What have you seen?"

"Where are you heading next?"

"How long will you be here?"

It had been over a decade since I had visited my home country, Australia. Much had changed, but much had also

116

remained the same, and I was interested in hearing what our fellow houseguests thought of Australia.

In response to my question, they smiled and said, "Australia is a beautiful country. It's so…civilized." They went on: "Great food, very clean, friendly, and safe."

While nodding in agreement, my heart swelled with pride that my home country measured up so well to these seasoned travelers.

After breakfast, we checked the time and quickly took our leave, knowing we had only a few minutes to finish packing and make it to the docks by launch time.

It was a dreary day; heavy clouds threatened to send lightning and chaos toward us, and we were met with the heavy rain and thunderstorms that had been predicted.

Driving toward the dock provided limited opportunity to see the beach, but the occasional glimpse provided a scene of crashing waves, white-tops as far as the eye could see, and roiling ocean waters.

I looked at Laura and said, "I hope this launch is a decent size...we are in for a rough crossing."

"We are going to need a bigger boat," I quipped as we pulled into the boat ramp and saw the small twenty-four foot outboard motorboat waiting for us. (Jaws remains one of the best fish stories ever, and I love to use that line!).

We arrived at the dock right on time at 9:20 a.m. and met our captain, Jason. A tall bronzed Australian, with a strong accent and typical Australian attitude ("She'll be right, mate!"), he took our bags and dropped them into the front of his boat (launch) as it bobbed up and down on the water. Of course, the dock was behind a seawall, which protected it from the turbulent waters we were about to cross.

Jason warned us that we would be in for a rough ride as we rounded the seawall: "We will have a few bumps at first as we go around that reef. There" he said, pointing to our right, "and then we will hug the beach as much as possible before making the crossing. I will try to get you there without you needing a chiropractor when you arrive. Stay seated, there are grab handles at each side, and the life jackets are under your seat. It may get a bit rough at times."

A passenger subject to the debilitating effects of seasickness would have been in trouble the minute we left the dock. Rounding the seawall, we were hit with the full force of the ocean, her four-foot swells lifting and dropping our launch mercilessly; causing it to bob like a cork.

It was exhilarating!

Neither Laura nor I suffer from the effects of motion sickness and found the rise and fall of the boat exciting. The bow dug into the swell-sending walls of saltwater over the bow and onto the heavy plastic squall sheets that surrounded the front of the boat, obliterating everyone's view for a few seconds.

The fifty-minute trip across to our island was filled with the sound of bumps, crashes, and roars of excitement as the boat lurched, dropped, and climbed the ocean swells.

Soon enough, we found safe harbor as the captain expertly navigated a series of rocks protruding from the sand of a small protected cove. The sandy beach was surrounded by palm trees; the white sand beckoned to us as I could only imagine the calls of the Sirens beckoning the sailors of old.

As Jason expertly guided his boat, he reminded us, "You are in Far North Queensland. These are tropical waters. We do have sharks and crocodiles, so I suggest to you that you refrain from swimming at night. Stinger season (a deadly jellyfish in tropical Australian waters) has started, and you would be really unlucky if one were to sting you here."

With those words ringing in our ears, we jumped off the stern into a few inches of warm, tropical water and met our caretaker, Chris, whose skin was like deep brown leather from too many hours in the hot tropical sun.

He showed us to our house, gave us a quick tour, and, before departing, said "Now, you may hear me blowing leaves away each day. I usually do it in the mornings. I like to do it each day because here on the island, we have a snake known as the 'death adder.' It is about twelve to eighteen inches long and likes to sleep in the leaves. It will probably only bite you if you step on it, but be careful, OK? It probably won't kill you if it bites you, but it will make you pretty sick."

Two warnings in the space of fifteen minutes reminded me of the truth of something I have known since I was a young boy – everything in Australia wants to kill you!

It took less than sixty seconds for that thought to leave me when I walked into the living room, an open air affair looking over the trees and down to the rocks surrounding the cove we landed on.

Thoughts of sharks, crocodiles, stingers and snakes were replaced instantly by the peacefulness that can only be found when nature in all its glory sneaks up and tells you to open your eyes.

In that moment, time became meaningless and life became *simple*.

We had made a conscious decision to unplug for a few days. After a week of family reunions in Melbourne, a short but awe-inspiring trip along the Great Ocean Road in Victoria, and a few days working together in Surfer's Paradise, Queensland, we now found ourselves here, in Far North Queensland, on an island with no clocks.

Time is not relevant here.

Life is driven by the geography of the landscape.

We allow ourselves to be tied only to the biological needs of the body, the movement of the sun, and the path of the moon across these endless skies. In fact, time *has* no meaning without these movements in the sky and without our biological patterns. Without these things, time has no meaning and no relevance beyond reminding *you* of what you *think* you need to do.

It was in North Queensland that I discovered I needed to write this book. But I want to keep my realization as simple as life without clocks.

Life can be hard.

And we, as humans, have a way of complicating everything we touch. In fact, if something is not complicated *yet*, we create ways to *make* it harder.

If something is simple, we don't believe it can be any good.

I feel like all people planning to become business owners should understand this one thing: life is simple. Not "life can be simpler" or "simplify your life."

Life is simple. Just that.

You can do it. It is now time to get started on becoming the business owner you always needed to become.

*Overwhelmed? Keep it simple – have questions? Send me your ideas, comments, questions or complaints. I want to know what you think. You can reach me at:*
*www.IAmNotFinished.com/contact-us*

# 11. Supercharge Your Success

My greatest wish right now is for you to step up, feed your inner entrepreneur, and move forward with confidence and intent; safe in the knowledge that you have a plan, a system, and a destination in mind.

I want you to be wildly successful. I want you go out there and follow your own path now that you know whether you should buy an existing business or build your own from scratch. There is nothing holding you back now…except yourself.

And the sad reality is that most people who read this book, even you, will respond in one of several ways:

-   You may call BS on the system. You may not accept the validity of the concepts and processes presented, and you may wish you had never invested the money getting the book. But mostly, you wish you could get back the time it took to read it. If this describes you, maybe you should just put the book up on a shelf, ignore the information, and move on your own way. My wish for you is that you, too, find a way to create great success.

-   You may see the benefit in some of the information presented. You may have even done some of the exercises and perhaps even created your personal blueprints. And they make for great thinking, but nothing more happens. You see value in the book and its processes but are not willing to turn them into action. Perhaps you have not overcome your fear (whether that is of failure or success). Your internal blocks are preventing you from moving forward, and you stay trapped in a battle with your inner entrepreneur. If this is you, remember that fighting with your inner entrepreneur will only keep you on a cycle of never owning your own business while always searching for a way to achieve that dream.

- Some people will do the exercises, will see the future, and will understand that action is what is needed most. You may start taking the steps that are needed and start the process of following your personal blueprint only to run out of energy over time. You may stumble and fall, and you may fail to move forward. You will drift back to old habits and struggle daily as you wish you had the dedication to see it through.

- A very small group of people will understand the process completely, will run with it, and will succeed beyond their wildest dreams as they follow the process. If this is you, you may buy (or build) your perfect business, use the processes in this book to run and manage your businesses, and will hopefully tell everybody who cares to listen that *this book* changed your life for the better.

So, let me ask you this – which group do you fall into?

Which group do you wish to be in?

My sister-in-law, Sandy, is a retired professional tennis player. For several years, she was seeded in the teens among all the world's best players. She attributes her success as a tennis player to her coach. It was her coach who kept her emotionally stable, fixed her game, her serve, her ground, and net game. She knew how to play tennis. Her natural skill and ability was far beyond the average player, but that was not enough to get her to the top twenty ranking worldwide.

All that knowledge and skill just meant she could hit a ball. Nothing more. So, what did her coach do? A whole lot of things she could not do for herself:

- Held her accountable for her actions, making sure she practiced every day, even when she didn't feel like it
- Identified the weaknesses in her game and helped her improve in those areas
- Built strategies so that the game was played to capitalize on her strengths and give her an advantage
- Kept her focused on the vison of the future that she had for herself
- Kept Sandy's health, relationships, and passion in a place of importance as her friend and mentor

But not any coach would have been successful. Sandy found an experienced coach, someone who understood not just the skills required of a top tennis player but a coach who could see "the gaps" that needed to be filled. This was a coach who could advise her on all aspects of the business that Sandy was in. Yes, tennis is a business too. (As a point of interest, Sandy's coach was recently inducted into the Women's Tennis Hall of Fame – an honor few coaches ever receive).

If you find yourself in any of the groups of readers that I have described above, have you considered working with a coach to help you move forward?

I have created and taught you a system that is simple to understand but, to many, is very difficult to follow.

Most people fail because they have not been trained in discipline. A lack of discipline will prevent the full benefits of this system from being realized and will undermine the confidence you need to continue moving forward and take steps that will lead to success.

The right coach will hold you accountable. He will give you deadlines for completion of projects and make sure you follow through with what you say you want to do. The right coach will encourage you when things get hard, help you as you learn new ways of thinking, and celebrate when you have breakthroughs.

Your biggest enemy right now is *you*.

You are the only thing standing between now and the future you have envisioned. The thing most likely to prevent you from getting to the end is lack of accountability. When you must rely on yourself and yourself alone to take the next step... well, it is much harder than it needs to be.

Let's think about this another way: fear is the greatest challenge you will have to overcome.

If you have followed the process, your confidence right now is likely to be higher than it ever has been in the past.

You *know* exactly where you are going and how you expect to get there, so fear of failure has diminished to the recesses of your mind. It has taken a back seat to confidence and has been relegated to history.

But what about fear of success?

Some people never move forward because they fear what success may do to them. They fear the impact on their relationships and their families. They fear the temptations that success may bring. The seduction of wealth is well known to those unprepared for it.

But why would you fear these things now? Your work throughout this process has identified your vision for the future, including your vision for your relationships. You have never been better prepared for success than you are today. That fear should also be banished because it is simply not real.

You know, I can tell you that I have been where you are right now. I can tell you how I felt, and I can describe the sleepless nights when I worried about whether I was good enough to do it.

I questioned everything many times.

Often, I had no answers. The only thing I could hold onto was my unyielding knowledge that my inner entrepreneur needed to be fed.

I wrote this book to help people just like you – people with that insatiable urge to own their own business. I wrote it to teach you some of the things that I learned along the way, things that simplify the process and make it easy to move forward.

I know that if you do everything here, you will be ready to buy or build the perfect business for yourself. I know that you have everything you need to become successful. It is all here.

But I also know that most people will get to their vision faster, easier, and more effectively if they work with a coach;

a coach with lots of experience, supported by a strong education.

I am asking you to fundamentality change the way you think about money. I know that this sort of change is really difficult to make and even harder to maintain.

I am asking you to prioritize your relationships and structure them the way *you* want them to be. This can easily become a source of greater stress, especially if your partner has different ideas. Sometimes, it may be very difficult to get your partner on board with these new ideas.

The temptation to quit will be very strong at times. A coach will get you through these difficult times and keep you focused on the important things.

There is one more thing we need to consider.

I have not discussed the need for an operational business plan thus far. It is a little outside of the parameters of this book and may form the foundation of my next book. I highly recommend that, regardless of whether you plan to build or buy, you diligently prepare an operational business plan that serves as a blueprint for your business as you plan your entry into the business world.

You can use the same techniques and principles that you used during this process. An operational business plan will help you organize your thoughts about how you intend to manage, grow and develop your business.

To summarize this chapter:

- You have all the information you need to do it by yourself

- Most people fail to own their own business because they lack the level of discipline needed to get through the tough spots
- A good coach will hold you accountable and will ensure discipline
- A good coach will see your "gaps" and help you find ways past them
- A good coach will get you there faster, easier and more efficiently than you can do yourself

At the end of the day, you will fail 100% of the times you don't try. You have this. You have the knowledge and the practical steps to get you there. I say it is time for you start building your operational plan while you search for the right business to buy or start building your own.

**Action is all you need now. Just action.**

# 12. Be the Action Hero

Without putting too fine a point on it (well, actually…this truly is the point of it all), today is decision day for you. You can continue on with the life you currently have, or you can take a giant leap of faith and make the decision to own a business of your own. As you read this book, you learned everything you need to know to be able to make the right decision for your business.

You learned how to envision your future, how to be honest with yourself, and how to create a blueprint to bridge the gap.

You learned how to think about money and how to arrange your finances to gain financial stability through a systematized approach. And you learned that you never need to worry about rent payments or car payments again if you follow the bucket system.

You learned how to build and maintain strong relationships that work for you, even while managing the stresses that come with business ownership.

You learned that emotional and physical health are paramount to your future success, and equally importantly, you learned that you may have to fill your skills and knowledge gaps as you move into business ownership.

You learned that your beliefs must be acknowledged and adhered to and that your passions will lead you to the best business for you.

You learned how to identify the best business type for you and know whether to build your own business or to buy an existing one.

You know the broad options available and how to identify which is best for your business ideas.

You learned how to find a business to buy at the best possible price and how to think about your start-up.

You learned a technique that can be used in all aspects of your life as you grow your business to logically work through finding the right solutions and paths forward.

You learned how to create a simple blueprint that will move you forward in every situation.

You learned that opportunity can be found amidst risk.

Now, there is only one thing left for you to do.

### It's Not the Danger That's Important, It's the Action

It was 1964, two months before my eighth birthday, and the world was in turmoil… The failed invasion of Cuba in 1961 was followed by the assassination of JFK in November 1963. The cold war was in full swing, and every sane American was searching for Russian spies.

But I didn't care.

At that moment, the world was something that I could see, touch, and bask in. It was summer, and I had no deeper thoughts than the sun, beaches, and, yes, the enjoyment of watching girls in bikinis walking along the shoreline, the gentle waves lapping at tanned legs as they strolled along. (I was starting to understand why my oldest brother was spending less time playing with me and far more time talking to the tanned bombshells that inhabited this beach resort every summer.)

With the arrival of the summer holidays, the population of Rosebud (a sleepy little beach resort a couple of hours' drive from Melbourne, Australia) would swell from a couple of thousand to tens of thousands of sun-worshipping beachgoers, the money in their pockets supporting the local community for the non-summer periods.

My family owned a small vacation house, nothing special, but it was a place that brought us kids a great deal of joy every summer when we would spend several weeks at the beach – swimming, playing, exploring.

The only thing more important than playing on the beach was the occasional visit to the local carnival. Every summer, the carnival lights would turn on, the music would blare, and the crowds would come. I recall watching the lights on the Ferris Wheel and the carnival rides, blinking and flashing … a cacophony of light, whirling endlessly among the faces of the children looking in awe at the scary rides (and wishing we were brave enough to try them).

But on this day, many decades ago, the carnival was silent.

But I didn't care about that, either.

I didn't give it a thought.

Nope. At that moment, my thoughts were echoing those of my brother's. He was just one year older than me and I idolized him.

"I wonder how deep it is?" he had asked me, earlier that day, when we had broken the rules…in a big way.

How deep could it be?

I was aware of the brilliantly hot sun as it baked my tanned skin. It was still morning, but the temperature was rising rapidly, ominously foretelling of record temperatures. The sun reflected from the water, making it impossible to see below the surface.

A few seagulls were circling, squawking loudly as they fought over a scrap of food they had found. The breeze was non-existent; an omen, perhaps?

Squinting against the sun's reflection, I could see the bottom…it wasn't that far! Squinting tighter – my eyes becoming dark slits in my darker tanned face – I could see a couple of small fish swimming along the bottom, a few strands of deep green seaweed seductively stroking the floor, and a small crab scurrying back to its hole in the sand.

"It's not deep," I yelled, as I stood and jumped over the side. We had taken our eldest brother's paddle board that morning.

While we had a great degree of freedom in our childhood, one of the rules that was inviolable was that we were not to take the paddle board out without adult supervision. It was too big for us. At around six feet long and two feet wide, the plywood board was too difficult for us to carry, even though it had handles. The layers of marine varnish kept the wooden board in seaworthy condition, but it made the board particularly slippery, especially when it was wet.

At eight and nine years of age, we lacked the physical size and strength to maneuver the beast out of the water. And on the water, we had to work as a team to move it, with Les taking the front, standing up and balancing as he used the paddles to propel us. I sat at the back, doing everything possible to keep it balanced.

On this day, we had discovered that if Les grabbed the front handle, and I grabbed the back, we could carry it short distances.

We took it to the beach.

We pushed it into the water.

We paddled furiously away from shore…and went further than we had ever been before – far further than any adult would have allowed us to go.

The water was colder than expected, causing me to nearly gasp and suck in a lung full.

It was much deeper, too.

Before I knew it, I was sitting on the bottom of the ocean, bubbles coming out of my mouth, eyes wide open as I surveyed the sea life … from under the sea.

My eyes followed the air bubbles. Up and up they went, and I remember seeing the shape of the paddle board way above me; the light of the sun creating a halo around its shape.

It was then that I realized that I was in trouble. Yes, I could swim a little and was comfortable in water…but I had never been this deep before, and I had never been this scared before.

Somewhere in the back of my mind, I knew I had a couple of choices, and that if I chose the wrong one, I may not survive:

- I could panic and flail my arms around, until my breath fully escaped, and I sucked in the relief that only a lung-full of water could bring, or…

- I could use all my strength to push up off the bottom and fight my way to the surface – a single objective, a single path, a drive to success.

When I broke the surface, gasping and coughing, my brother looked down at me and said, "Well, that looked like fun! Did you enjoy the view?"

Clambering back onto the paddle board, laughing and coughing at the same time, I had no idea that this event would be so important to my life. After all, we were just kids doing something dumb, right?

Was I ever really in danger?

To this day, I have no idea. How deep was it? If you asked me back then I would have said, "five miles," but today… Maybe it was only ten feet, maybe twelve?

You see, it is not the danger, or even the perceived danger that is important here; it is the action.

And I learned that day, and many days since, that the decisions we make can make a huge difference to the direction of our life.

But making a decision is only half the story – it is the action that follows that makes the difference.

We can make decisions all day long. It is easy to decide that we will pay off our credit cards. It is much harder to do it. It is easy to decide we will spend more time with our family, but it is much harder to do it.

You have the tools to make it easy to make decisions…but do you have the will to take the action?

Are you going to flail around under a sea of fear, an ocean of doubt, your arms thrashing violently as you try to subdue the inner entrepreneur that is seeking release; eventually succumbing to a life that lacks the purpose that you were born for?

Or, are you ready to push back, to take purposeful action, to use every skill you have learned and practiced to rise to the surface and laugh as you realize you can do it?

You have done it…you are on your way to your destination. You are on your way to the purpose that you were born into.

You are on your way to owning your business.

My wish for you is that you will not leave this book on a shelf, gathering dust and waiting to be discarded when you go back to the life you already have.

My wish is that you will use it every day and that you will practice the skills. I hope that you will take strong action on a daily basis.

My wish for you is that you release your inner entrepreneur, knowing that you now have the skills and knowledge to make it happen.

My wish for you is that you find a business coach to guide you along the path to success.

My coaching program goes into greater detail on each of the areas in this book, and ensures you have a written, detailed operational business plan completed and ready to go by the end of the program. I would love to work with you to make your dreams happen.

If you choose to work with me, and I choose you as a client, your journey:

- Will not accept excuses
- Will require personal accountability
- Will require responsibility
- Will get you ever closer to that abundant, financially stable life you want.

Break on through to the other side…

### *You will be a business owner!*

*To discover more about my coaching program, and to apply for a limited number of spaces, go to IAmNotFinished.com/apply*

*Have a question for me? Send me your ideas, comments, questions or complaints. I want to know what you think. You can reach me at:*

*www.IAmNotFinished.com/contact-us*

# About the Author

Randy Baker is on a mission...a big mission...to coach clients on how to find, buy, or build the perfect business for them.

His hands-on and sometimes folksy approach to disrupting industries has proven successful across verticals, including aerospace, the early internet, and, most recently, cryptocurrency.

From selling fish, to being kidnapped, surviving polio, and rubbing elbows with the giants of industry, he has lived nine lives and has a story for every situation. His story-centric, dynamic approach to building and operating companies has allowed him to change the world in substantive ways. And he's just getting started.

His experience as a hands-on operations and finance leader for rapidly growing, distressed, or start-up organizations – coupled with the knowledge gained by starting and exiting several businesses of his own – is now available to you so that you don't have to make the mistakes he made.

Randy received his Bachelor of Business from the Royal Melbourne Institute of Technology and is a Chartered Accountant. His early career at KPMG provided the strong foundation for his business career. Living and working on three continents and traveling through over a hundred countries gives Randy a rounded perspective on life and business.

He believes that everyone is born with a purpose and that some are born to be entrepreneurs. Helping clients find their inner entrepreneur and launching their own business is his passion and purpose.

Australian by birth and American by choice, Randy lives with his wife Laura in Austin, Texas. He can be found on sunny days taking in the rays in his classic Mustang convertible or sipping a red on his patio while steaks sizzle on the grill.

# Thank You

You've finished reading this book! You rock!

I know you are on the way toward buying or building the perfect business for you. I want to support you as much as possible as you move forward.

Visit my website, IAmNotFinished.com and schedule a free discussion where we can discuss how you can best find the confidence to take the action that makes a difference and keeps you on the path to success.

I'm passionate about helping people find, buy, or build the perfect business. Please send any feedback to me. I would love to hear your story!

*Have a question for me? Send me your ideas, comments, questions or complaints. I want to know what you think. You can reach me at:*

*www.IAmNotFinished.com/contact-us*